Beijing Diary

北 京 日 记

Beijing Diary

北京日记

An East-West Love Story

Bess Spero Li

Bonus Books, Inc., Chicago

93   92   91   90   89   5   4   3   2   1

International Standard Book Number: 0-933893-99-X

Bonus Books, Inc.
160 East Illinois Street
Chicago, Illinois 60611

Chinese characters by Eunhee Choe

Printed in the United States of America

*To Ruo-xin, without whom
the spirit of this journal
would not be as it is*

Contents

Dear Reader,

    In 1982, I went to China as a foreign student. I was 21 years old. The following pages reflect the journal that I kept while living there.

    As you read, I ask that you keep this thought in mind: described here is how one young woman experienced China. Although the impact of a few thousand years of history continues, the China of today is very different from what it was in 1982.

    No country, no person is static.

    China is no exception. Neither is the young woman.

Bess Spero Li
February 1989

Part I

中國

*China
1982–83*

August 23, 1982   *At sunset*

At long last, I'm on my way. All around me, the faces of Asians. They are flying home but not me! Home will be very far away this year.

Looking out over the wing, there stretches a sea of deep purple, with a red rose on its border. And here I sit, on my way to China. Well, kiddo, you've done it! I am no less than thrilled.

An hour ago, sweat was running down my back as I waited at the departure gate. After dragging my bags halfway around the L.A. airport from Imperial to Philippine Airlines, I was greeted by a swarm of smiling Asians, carting children and boxes, milling about—and they didn't seem disturbed by the long wait. They were laughing and talking to each other. Their patience was quite catching. Though I couldn't understand a word, I returned their friendly expressions of greeting, got my ticket, and then made my way to the gate. Called Jan in L.A., to say goodbye. She was as excited as I was. Tufts seems ages away. I can picture the hill in my mind, Carmichael all lit up, Fletcher, et al. Sweet times—but I have been waiting for this day for a year and a half now. I miss you, Cath, but I have no regrets.

A quick stop in San Fran, my brother Joey's city. There's nothing quite like flying at night. San Francisco is aglow. Christ, I must be dreaming. I can't help but recall dancing at the bar at the top of the hub in Boston, looking out over the town, my town for three years. And now I wonder, what does Hong Kong look like at night? Or Beijing? Soon to find out!

Wednesday, August 25   *2:00 pm*
    Manila

(No entry for Tuesday because it was only a few hours long.)

Fifteen-hour flight—mostly in darkness. We slept (not too badly, either) and ate every four hours. Christ, I must have gained a ton. Sat next to a Filipino missionary and the son of the former owner of Manila's *Free Press*. Free, that is until Marcos nailed it, apparently. The story he told was a sad one, not so much about his own family's trouble under Marcos, but the depression the rest of the island was experiencing while Lady Marcos was building palaces and flying to New York City every week. I looked at him for a long time as he slept. He was returning home after finishing business school at Harvard, coming home to God knows what. He didn't know himself, this sweet, skinny rich man's son. As I stared at him in the darkness, I could only imagine what color the world had been painted for him: a glorious bright blue, with a splash of dirty gray tossed over it because of one man. It's embarrassing to recall how vehemently Mr. Reagan supports Marcos. Crazy damn world.

My first taste of Southeast Asia is Manila. We had an eight-hour layover here. We were given accommodations at a nearby hotel. I signed my name and received a room key. I suddenly realized I was traveling. Basha, traveling alone in Southeast Asia. Mixed feelings, which I succeeded in squelching by washing my face and taking a look at the map I found in the room. The hotel is comfortable but tacky. Not plastic—just mediocre. Everything is steeped in the tropical humidity. The restaurant had cold food with "Yes, ma'am/No ma'am" waitresses. Americanized. Yuk. I think a day is all I'd give it here, even if I had the choice.

Can't wait to get out of Manila. I can't help but think of Vietnam as I look around me—it really looks like Saigon and I feel like the ugly American, as much as I try to smile and be courteous. They treat us as if we were the masters and they were slaves, with a bitter sort of a feeling mixed in.

We leave for Hong Kong in a few hours. I'm anxious and, yes, a bit apprehensive, to be truthful. I picture Hong Kong as a sea of Chinese faces and flashing neon signs. Chaos.

As I sit writing, the rain is beginning to come down over the waving palm trees outside my window. The nasal sounds of some Chinese dialect can be heard from the hallway. Christ, will these allergies never go away?

Tacky purple-and-blue wallpaper in the room here. American music, mostly disco. Is this Southeast Asia? No, Basha, just a part of it.

A guy who I met during this stopover told me that he saw Pepsi signs even as he and his friends floated down the Amazon. America is everywhere. It's wild! Really—it's a shame. What were these cultures like before we came along?

Must catch the bus to the airport. Can't wait to get there.

August 21, 1982   *7:15 am*
    Hong Kong
    I woke up on the island of Hong Kong this morning. Amazed.
Upon arrival at the airport last night, I found my way to a taxi (customs was a snap, they didn't even open my luggage) and sat, gaping
at the city as the driver sped along, dodging pedestrians. Many a
near miss!
    Aaron and Phillip, two of the students in our group of eleven for-
eign students going to Beijing, were here already. I'm sure they were
greatly amused by the look on my face, which was one of sheer de-
light and fatigue all at once. First impressions aren't the most reli-
able, as I have certainly proven in my day, but these two guys seem
quite nice—laid back, friendly, interested, fairly rational. Carol finally
arrived, full of energy and a smile, thankful to see Phillip. I won't forget how she came down the hall when she arrived and called to him.
He leaped up and went to greet her. It must be a different perspective, walking through the streets of Hong Kong with someone you
love as opposed to alone. For me, there's enough to overwhelm me
without a lover to add to it. Still, they look happy.
    I couldn't sit around for long. We ventured out into the Hong
Kong night, which was hot and a bit sticky. None of us cared, though.
It was a thrill to be here, sweat or no sweat.
    Introduction to Hong Kong: the night outdoor market. Ten inter-
connecting blocks were teeming with people and lined with—well,
practically anything one could want.
    The food. There was very little that I recognized, actually. No
egg roll-type things. But shrimp and octopus fried in batter, cooked
nuts, fruits fitting all descriptions, noodles, hot tea, thousand-year-
old eggs, herbs for medication—on and on. I was astounded. Everyone stared at us, just about as much as we stared. One old man came
up and pointed to Phillip's red beard and laughed. I guess they're not
used to red hair.
    The market had more than just food. There were tacky Ameri-
can shirts and sneakers, old radios, knick knacks, and other things.
More fascinating than the objects being sold were the sellers themselves. They either stood behind their store stands or sat on the
ground, calling out their inventories to attract the passersby. I felt
quite odd, actually. Carol warned me that I would soon get used to being stared at. They were fascinated by us.

Around ten-thirty, we went to a little restaurant on the same block as the marketplace. My comrades spared me the agony of ordering food on my first night in Asia, thank God. After a bit of confusion we ordered dumplings and a few bottles of beer.

The little kids were so adorable I wanted to squeeze them all. There's nothing like a little Chinese toddler having playtime with a long soup noodle. I didn't have my camera with me, but today I'll get some shots of those sweet little devils.

I must be a little off kilter, because I woke up last night to find myself standing in front of the closet door, feeling around the inside as if I were looking for something. I would have laughed at myself if I hadn't been so sleepy. I just went to the bathroom and back to sleep.

We woke up early—both of us too excited to sleep any later. Aaron stayed in my room since we thought Phillip and Carol might like to be together after being apart for so long—which they did. Aaron and I didn't mind.

We're off to meet the rest of the clan!

4:15 that afternoon

Had to leave in the middle of this entry. What a day. If this place weren't so fascinating, lively, and full of color, the heat really would have been unbearable. But, no problem. The ferry over to Hong Kong from Kowloon was gorgeous. The harbor itself was scummy, but the contrast of the old wooden boats against the modern shoreline of Hong Kong with its white skyscrapers was really quite a sight.

Conversations turn often to Beijing, soon to be our new home. As some realized that McDonalds wouldn't be around they suddenly had a "Big Mac attack." I was persuasive, however, and managed to convince a few to come with me to a little corner place for strange stir-fried vegetables and soup with noodles. The best part was the cold orange juice, believe it or not. I wandered around after lunch, exchanged money at the bank, and met some Americans there who were on their way to Nanking. Exciting times. I'm glad to see young people adventurous, open-minded, and on the move; excited, ready to experiment, positive and highly motivated. During the last six months at school, I was beginning to wonder if those kind existed anymore, besides my close friends, and Cath—and Nathan, at times. They're both sleeping soundly right now. Dream of me, sweet Nathan. I almost miss you.

Hong Kong is a strange mixture of old and new. Amid the shining, classy bank buildings walk businessmen in their suits, right alongside peddlers, street corner shoemakers, and women with sacks of nuts and fruit on their backs. Some of those of the old world are barefoot or blind, wearing thin, shabby grey clothing. And then there are the younger people, well dressed in bright colors and high fashion. Once again, there's something wonderful about contrast.

Sunday, August 29, 1982
  Canton, at the White Cloud Hotel

We have an unanticipated two-day stay over here on the way to Beijing. This is a Chinese holiday, so all the trains from here to Beijing are full until Tuesday. Oh well! We're in no rush.

Yesterday morning I woke up early to walk around Hong Kong one more time. It's a different city at six o'clock in the morning, of course. Finally, on the train—what a trip! The first leg of the journey, which took us to Lo Wu, the border station, was an old fashioned–type train with open windows, no air conditioning. Hot as the hubs of hell. But we had hand fans, which helped. Sipped on some strange sweet juice as we rolled along to the border. When we hit customs, they gave us water and shuffled us past the long lines of Chinese to the customs area. Our first taste of segregation. They put us on a separate on the train and a separate waiting area at the border—as if we had a disease. The disease of Western thought.

And finally, it appeared: the sign at the end of the station that said "To China." Elated. Beneath the sign stood the beautiful Chinese guards. We all were grinning like zanies, so they couldn't help but smile at us. I stepped across the bridge, which was the border, into China. It's no exaggeration to say that things changed radically once we crossed over. The people on the Mainland are much friendlier than those on Hong Kong.

The girl who makes the beds came in. My Chinese is improving already; three days ago I wouldn't have been able to understand or have that conversation. Now that makes me feel better. At breakfast this morning, we coaxed one of the waiters to sit down and talk with us. They're all so friendly and relaxed that the atmosphere was very conducive to chatting and laughing, passing the time.

On the train up to Canton, we passed through the most beautiful agricultural areas I've ever seen. The Chinese seem to be such meticulous farmers. The method they use makes the green hills look like stairs carpeted with velvet. Dotting the green fields are wide Chinese huts, water buffaloes, and men and women carrying baskets on their backs. We passed a watering hole where a few little boys were sharing the swimming pleasures with a few water buffaloes.

As the scenery passed by, the tears welled up in my eyes. Silly girl. But finally I'm here. I felt relieved, I guess. So many people had told me it was impossible to get here—but here I am! They even played cheerful Chinese music to accompany our first voyage through China's southern communes. It was gorgeous.

Finally, in Canton, we all felt a little depressed that we had to stay for three nights. We're anxious to get to Beijing. But after a shower and a good dinner, we realized, what could be bad? And so it is Canton that we shall explore for now. Though the city itself has not stood out, the people have been unusually friendly, not concerned with appearing sophisticated and aloof, especially compared to my comrades in the States. Sweet family of mine, I wish you could experience the natives here. It doesn't sound real when I write it down, and that frustrates me.

I want to go out and get a newspaper to see what's happening in the world. And off now to explore this town!

August 31, 1982

On the train to Beijing.

It's about seven o'clock in the morning by now. We boarded the train at nine o'clock last night. Absolutely jubilant. Sweaty, but jubilant.

We are riding the hard seat to Beijing, along with a carload of Chinese who are getting a kick out of us. Phillip just came over to say that the train just ran over and killed a peasant—that was the large jolt I felt a few minutes ago. Jesus. They say he was a young man.

I slept well last night. The rocking of the train was gentle and the night air smelled like China. The windows that line the walls of the car are always open, so fresh breezes blew in to keep us cool. And we're in China! What could be bad? Before most of us went to sleep, we took the opportunity of being confined together to get to know each other. Mark talked to me for a long time about his experiences in Taiwan. For him, it was very frustrating. The people were caught up in materialism, their business; anything outside of that was not important. He described it as a sort of complacency, as they were caught up in their materialistic existence. Sounds like the town I come from. Mark's a very interesting guy. He speaks Chinese quite well. Also spent his senior year of high school in Kenya. He said he had been angry and bitter about the U.S., and the attitudes that make up our culture. So he looked abroad for a new perspective, new ideas. His bitterness, he says, has mellowed. In the meantime, he has fallen in love with China.

The communes with the peasants already out in the field look like picture postcards. It is gorgeous country. So far, the people have been equally beautiful—in spirit. Our stay in Canton really pointed out to me the positive attitude the people seem to have. They all have a goal: to make China a better place. They work hard and in the meantime enjoy one another's company.

On one of my walks through the backyard of the city, I stopped for something to drink. My favorite, an orange soda. It's the national drink. The store where I bought it was a little stand by the side of the road, like the rest of them. As I was contemplating the question of whether or not to sit down among the natives, one of them said in English, "Please sit down." I was rather surprised, to say the least, but I accepted and sat down beside him.

Christ, here I was, in China, sitting next to a Chinese man who was eager to talk to me about my country and his. It was really a trip. It turns out, he's a physics professor at the Technological Institute in Canton. Soon a crowd had gathered, and they watched us converse. The man was proud to tell me that his uncle owns the store we were sitting in front of. He told me the word for "private" in Chinese. The government apparently only takes 7 yuan from the store's profits each month. His uncle makes a profit of 5 fen on each bottle he sells. Yes, the times they are a-changin'.

Soon an hour had gone by and I knew I had to start finding my way home before it got dark. I thanked him for the pleasant conversation. His uncle timidly asked me if I would take his picture. Taking pictures is difficult in China; people are often afraid of having their pictures taken and some are quite offended when you snap a picture of them without asking. So I was pleased to have this opportunity to take a picture that wasn't a risk.

I walked home slowly, enjoying the end-of-the-day atmosphere as everyone rode their bicycles home from work. It is at this hour when the marketplace is most lively. Piles of fish, vegetables, and fruit are quickly depleted as the Chinese buy their evening meal. It was quite a scene.

Breakfast this morning was eggs on thick pieces of toast. I think I've gained a least six pounds already since I arrived in Asia. They eat so much starch and grease. One of the women in the group, Cary, won't eat most of the stuff, but as a result she has little or no energy to walk around and travel. As for me, I eat what I need to keep running. So far my stomach is fine. Round, but fine.

We stopped for a moment in Changsha and I got off the train to get some air. The train car smells like a barn and it gets harder to breathe as the day gets hotter. Still, I haven't heard any children screaming. I looked over to the next set of bunks and saw a young couple singing Chinese songs. By the looks of them, I thought they were from Hong Kong. In conversation with them later, I found out that I was correct. They were on their way to China for a visit.

Canton will always be a special place to me. The three days we spent there, my first days on the Mainland, were packed with discovery and excitement. But most of all, I felt comfortable enough to wander the streets and chat with the people when I could find the right words. Traveling around the city by myself was frightening at first, but I got over the fear as soon as I found that the Chinese were eager to talk to me and help me find my way around.

It seems as if the whole country is under construction. Everywhere one looks one can see building sheds surrounded by bamboo scaffolding. This scaffolding is said to be as sturdy as steel, but of course much lighter and faster to assemble. It bends with the breeze but doesn't break.

"What are you writing about?" Bob asks me. Sweet boy. Manchild. He is on this trip with his girlfriend, Cary. In one way, it must be nice to have someone there, someone you know will explore with you and always endure the stares with you. My loneliness really got to me the night before last. But I was snapped out of it in a sweet way. Something possessed me to go upstairs to the dance hall to see what the Chinese danced like after being forbidden to dance until two and a half years ago. They were dancing to music from about thirty years ago. They stepped to the waltzes like beginners carefully, cautiously. Much to my surprise, a young man walked over to me and asked me to dance. I hadn't been there but five minutes. A Chinese man asking an American woman to dance? That's a good sign. He gently took my hand and we walked up to the dance floor. I was a bit apprehensive, afraid that I might do or say something that would offend him, in such a *touchy* situation. But he was so pleased to be dancing with a foreigner that I could have stepped on his toes and he would have smiled. He spoke fairly good English. And wouldn't you know it, the last song we danced to was "Tenderly," Mom's favorite.

I'm tired. The big breakfast wore me out. They have piped in some pleasant Chinese music. That helps. Knowing me, it won't take too long to fall asleep. I'm in China—and I haven't felt so pleased in ages. Shit, I stink like a construction worker. Might as well get used to it.

September 3, 1982   *Friday*
   Beijing Shi Fan University

I can hear the sound of the train whistle in the distance. Though it was a trying ride, it was exciting and well worth the sweat and discomfort. If only because it gave us a clear entry into northern China, so different from the South.

I woke up early on the morning of our arrival. Christ, after all this time. I was about to step off one lousy old train onto Beijing ground. Who could sleep?

Flash into my mind's eye: Saying goodbye to Mom and Dad at the airport, all of us tears in our eyes, smiling and thrilled, but sad. And today I wonder, how long will I stay here? A year to begin to learn the language and a year to use it, solidify it, read the newspaper, and talk to the people; perhaps two years is what it takes, not one. Crazy thoughts so early in the semester.

At any rate, the campus is a bit run-down, construction everywhere with red brick buildings lining the mud roads. Everywhere, the Chinese students are walking around. Classes began today for them.

I went to breakfast this morning after a pretty fair sleep. The pillow, however, seems to be filled with beans and the bed is harder than "extra-firm with a board" would be. Breakfast was a sweet cake, for me. They also served soft boiled eggs and fried types of dough. I still have the pip, which I picked up on the train, so I didn't feel like eating too much. On the way back to the dorm, a Chinese boy stopped me. He was trying to find out the American name of a magazine that he only knew in Chinese. I think it was *Forbes*. But we got onto the subject of economics and philosophy, both of which he is interested in. He knew about Friedman and Keynes and helped me read a bit of the newspaper. Nice guy. We must get together, he said, and compare ideas and ask questions. I would like to. Must study for the written exam. It's for placement here. I had the oral exam this morning. I really didn't do too badly. They're such friendly folks. All the people running this place seem quite laid back and while they are here, their time is for you, the student.

Finally, back to the dorm. One professor showed me the proper stroke order for my Chinese name. Carol showed me how to use a Chinese dictionary. One step at a time.

September 5, 1982   *Sunday evening*

There are a few Japanese girls down the hall on my floor. They are so nice. They sit down with us at meal times, smile and eat, talk among themselves, and smile at us. Their Chinese is almost nil, their English is almost nil—so we can't say much. One girl has been especially friendly and she seems as if she really wants to talk. We always say *Ni Hao* (hello) to one another, but that's the extent of it. So tonight when she was washing clothes in the laundry room, I stopped in to tell her in Chinese that there were so many things I wanted to say to her but I didn't yet know how to say them. We struggled for ten minutes but I couldn't get her to understand, because she had had so little Chinese. We smiled and I squeezed her arm, trying to tell her that I hated the isolation as much as she did and wanted badly to break the communication barrier. Soon—soon—just have patience.

Damn this chest cold! Got my first letter from Cath today. It took three weeks to get here! The tears came. I miss her so. Someone outside is singing on the street. They're laughing. Sweet people.

Must prepare for class. Nathan's letter will have to wait!

September 6, 1982

There are hard times, too. I came down with bronchitis and feel really depressed about it. The shots of penicillin that last a full painful minute and a half don't help. God damn these lungs, the bane of my existence. But everyone came to my rescue, held me tight, Harry's arms around my waist, sitting with me at the infirmary. I won't soon forget the scene of about eight of us sitting in Phillip's room, trying to decide what medicine I should take and Dianne standing there putting Vicks VapoRub on my chest, which was searching for a drop of air.

Dianne and Aaron went out for dinner and brought me back a whole tin of chocolates, the kind we all went crazy over the other night. Dianne's such a sweet woman.

I'm breathing easily now, only my back hurts and my mind feels a bit depressed. Mark, Rhoda, and Amy managed to crack me up at dinner. That was a riot. And they were playing classical Chinese music over the loudspeakers outside. Just like I played my stereo back at Tufts.

The penicillin shot tonight hurt like hell and I am angry that I got sick.

Classes started today. I'm very impressed at how animated and charismatic the professors are! The man is just like an actor from the Beijing opera and I can't take my eyes off of him. He's a wonderful teacher, as is the younger woman. And we don't speak a word of English. Amen. In a year or two, I may have this language down pat!

But first, must get well. Too tired to describe the infirmary.

September 8, 1982

Got up early this morning to do Tai Ji Quan (shadow boxing). My alarm went off at six o'clock, just a few moments before the school loudspeakers played the wake-up call music outside. By the time I had my sweats on and had gotten downstairs, the Chinese students were already out on the exercise courts, doing their morning routine to the music. It really was quite a sight. They all seemed to be in fairly good condition, doing fifteen minutes of exercise and twenty minutes of running. I had to wonder, what motivates them? Exercise, study, nap in the afternoon—perhaps these things all together give them high spirits. They seem so proud to be working hard, stretching their bodies without inhibition, proud of the results of hard work and hard studying.

The Tai Ji teacher was a beauty himself. Perfectly built and in perfect control of his body. Really a pleasure to watch. This being my first lesson in Tai Ji, it makes me think of my dancing years back in junior high. In touch with the body. Balance, grace. Tai Ji is a fluid set of movements, beautiful to watch and challenging to perform properly. The explanation was, of course, completely in Chinese. I caught a word here and there, but not much. For the most part, I simply imitated as best I could, yet I know there were certain innuendos, details that he was explaining that I missed because couldn't understand what he was saying. Patience, Basha, patience.

I can honestly say I missed home today. I think the isolation inherent in a foreigner's existence here is giving me a hard time. I find it frustrating to be walking in the midst of all the Chinese students and still be completely separated from their world. Once again, with my limited vocabulary there is very little I can say to them. Hence, I am cut off. It got really depressing today.

I got my fifth shot of penicillin at the infirmary today and they tried to tell me something, yapping away. I couldn't catch a word of it so I just said, "I don't understand," turned around and left. Went for a long walk to the yogurt man. It was good to get out and around. Soybean yogurt—nothing quite like it.

Dianne, my roommate, has just reminded me that tomorrow we will have been here for one week. It seems like months. I just put Pat Metheny on the tape deck, but that made me feel even worse. The U.S. is very far away from this place. It's not that I want to be there, but I'd love to see my family and Nathan and Cathy for a few days, just to recharge my battery. Oh, well. Fortunately, this group of Americans here is a special one. They've got the spirit, and their smiles or sarcastic jokes, a hug, and the taste of home that they bring to me help a lot during the tougher moments.

Today during my walk I saw a women breastfeeding her baby as they both sat on the curbside. No one seemed to be bothered by it. Boys walked home from school, arm in arm. Beautiful. They stared at me as I ate my yogurt in front of the store. It was a hard day.

Class, however, was excellent. My conversation class was dynamite, as usual. A true actor, he is. Somehow, he has us reading stories aloud when a week ago I would never have imagined we could. It's magic. Reminds me of French class with Jackie. For the first time in ages, since Jackie's class, Professor Dong has made me feel as if teaching is a worthwhile profession, and a stimulating challenge. What a feeling to create an atmosphere that will sweep up the students and wind them into the web of the learning process, only to emerge with fresh, new knowledge gleaned by way of excitement, creativity, and a bit of endurance. He is marvelous. If I could be sure that I could be as fine a mentor, I'd teach, too.

I met a man at dinner last night who edited some Chinese dictionary with Professor Klein. It's a small world—even smaller among Chinese studies scholars.

Must sleep. It is there that I find contentment during these days of transition and adjustment. In my waking hours, it only comes and goes—and rarely these past few days.

Everything is covered with dust, including my lungs. Too much rice, my tummy is round.

September 9, 1982

Just returned from tutoring. It actually was quite an unusual hour and a half, besides the usual "How do you use this word?" and all that. Amy and I sat at two wooden desks. Cement walls, cement floor. Our professor comes from a peasant family. Apparently her parents are still in the countryside. She teaches here and her husband works in a factory nearby. They have one child, a girl. She is short and round, with a typical peasant's face, yet a bit fatter than most Chinese I've seen. We read a story aloud about a greedy man who got nailed for not being content with what he had, for asking for more than his neighbors had. I think my tones are improving. Finally we had no more questions. I don't know where I found the nerve, but I asked her if she wanted to have another child. "No," she said firmly. And then she launched into an explanation of why, of what the government provides if you have only one child, and of what it does not provide if you have more than one. The incentives are quite clear. It is a good life if one has a single child.

Finally got my bicycle! I went into the city (about fifteen minutes by bus—slow bus) with two of the Japanese girls who live on my floor. Of the forty people in the dorm, thirty are Japanese. They know a few words of English and a little less Chinese than I know—so we can communicate, with a little help from pantomime, dictionaries, and a lot of smiling and laughing and bowing. They're such considerate people.

So, we hopped on the bus, one tall, funny-looking American and two short, cute little Japanese girls. What a sight we were. At the bicycle shop (once we found it in the mass of people, shops, and fruit stands), we found what we wanted and launched into the process of adjusting the nuts and bolts (apparently they come off the assembly line in poor shape) and changing the height of the seat. This took about forty-five minutes and we got a lesson in the parts of a bicycle in Chinese. Yoko bought popsicles and we gobbled them up—the only cold, wet anything you can find in Beijing on a hot day like today. I also wanted a basket. I don't know why, but one of the girls who was selling the bikes walked with me down the street to help me buy a basket. After that, with many thank yous, smiling, and goodbyes we dove into the Chinese traffic for the first time. Why there aren't forty accidents and forty deaths a day, I don't know. Everyone is always ringing their bells, buses honking their horns, and people darting in and out across the streets. It is no less than complete chaos. With many near-misses we made our way back to the school. They had never experienced this in Tokyo, nor had I ever navigated in a sea of bicycles such as this in Chicago, so we were simply thankful to make it home. The streets of the university were peaceful. The five o'clock sunlight gave a softness to the tree-lined lane and the music played sweet and Chinese over the loudspeakers. It was a gorgeous scene. And it was at that time, riding along, that I taught my Japanese friends how to say "beautiful"—in English first, then in Chinese.

That's what the day was, simply beautiful.

September 11, 1982

Went to the Great Wall today. What a spectacular thing. I still can't believe the Chinese built it—and that they thought it would really keep the enemy out. As it turned out, the Mongols snuck in through an unguarded place and that ended the impenetrability of the wall.

What a climb it was to get up to a high peak. My lungs are not in the best condition right now and it was tough going at times. But the view was worth the struggle, that's for sure. I met some Chinese from Shanghai during the climb. They were in Beijing on business. We spoke a combination of Chinese and English. Talked with them about Szechwan when the youngest of the bunch told me that he was there. They felt, as I do, that I must see Szechwan, an important province that has turned out some dynamic leaders and successful agricultural experiments. Perhaps that will be the second dialect I'll learn. Now Basha, learn Mandarin, first. Christ, my vocabulary is *small.*

We came home tonight, exhausted and sweaty. From the wall to two different sets of Ming Tombs, a bouncing bus ride, we were pretty tired and the shower never felt so good. I combed my hair, decided to let it hang loose at dinner time. Did I get the stares from the Chinese! Even wore my American clothes. I haven't felt beautiful in days, but as I walked out into the evening, I felt wonderful. Rode my new bicycle to the yogurt shop to meet Phillip and Carol and Bob and Cary. Riding the bicycle on the street helped me to step over the isolation barrier just a bit. It's nice to ride along with the Chinese, enjoying their mode of transportation. "I like to ride, oh yeah." Great song.

At the store, the first of an experience I'm sure will happen many times. A young man (as it turned out he's twenty-seven) sat down next to me, introduced himself in English, and said he is a medical student at the college nearby. We began to talk (he was no less than beautiful), he using English, I using as much Chinese as I could, when before I knew it, a crowd of at least forty people had gathered around us. They watched us closely and attentively, as if they were watching a particularly good movie. Then they stood and *stared* as we talked. *He* didn't seem to mind. I, however, was flipped out by it. I didn't expect to have that kind of reaction, but it's a strange feeling to be set on display when it's not on purpose. I wasn't acting for an audience as one does in a play. This was real life. And still, this crowd gathered, fascinated. I felt a bit ill at ease and my Chinese acquaintance must have sensed it. "Don't worry," he said reassuringly, "the Chinese people are very friendly." He was an interesting young man, and gentle, so I tried to ignore the crowd. When that didn't work, I decided I would feel better if I formally recognized their presence and I began to talk with them as well. I felt better after that. He was right; the Chinese people are very friendly.

Some pretty neat things are happening to me these past few weeks. I mean in the sense of personal things. I've never felt more independent and confident in my life. And now, I push myself less to be these things. They seem to be coming naturally. I tend to do things that make me feel good, feel comfortable, since I am the only one who will take care of myself here—for the most part. I feel less compunction to become close to people so quickly. I enjoy the adventure alone—perhaps even more. I can already see that a very close relationship could easily develop between Mark and me, but I will not let it happen. Independence, being free without ties, able to venture out on my own—that's crucial this year. And I love it. I'm glad to be bringing me along—she does well by me. *Acceptance is key.* My own acceptance of me, my mind, my shape, my enthusiasm, my habits. *Relaxation is key.* I know it sounds strange, but I must write it down because I've been thinking it ever since I came here. I felt—and feel now—a sense of relief upon arriving here to live for a year or two. And that really makes sense if I think about it. It's been two years of planning and thinking, applying, rejection, exploring, asking questions, hitting dead ends, making lists, figuring out money, on and on, never really knowing if all this would ever materialize! But finally, it has.

Amen. "Amen to that fair prayer, say I!" So comes the relief. It worked out. I'm here. And the effects have been wonderful.

Yes, I miss home. Mom and Dad, my two brothers Peter and Joe, and my sister-in-law Sally. Christ, how I miss them. But I feel calmer, more able. It is reflected in my everyday life. My enthusiasm comes through smoothly instead of awkwardly, and I feel at ease about it; not stifled or strange as I so often felt at school. I don't think it's China, per se. Perhaps it's a combination of timing, the people in the program, the Chinese attitude of friendliness and gentleness, and simply being away from the U.S.—*far* away. All these things. Perhaps even diet! I'm eating enough to feel satisfied. The Chinese diet is so healthy. That, too, could be key. Who knows?

Perhaps it's also this. There has almost always been a man in my life for the past three years, except for the few months before Nathan. I always felt just a bit confined, to varying degrees, loving it and despising it. Now, I am without a man at my side. My thoughts are no longer constantly distracted, preoccupied with thoughts of "him." I no longer have to conjure up thoughts of some "him" to feel happy. It is no longer the warm, loving soul lying next to me at night that makes me feel so good in the morning, and so content when I sleep and study. It is only me, and of course the people around me—but to a lesser extent as far as their influence compared to, for example, Nathan's influence.

It feels so good to be free. I feel like me. I make conscious decisions and feel good about the choice. At times I get positive responses from comrades that I know I deserve. I finally feel my feet are back on the ground. It's been a long time.

I have been in Beijing for only a week. Slowly, it is beginning to agree with me. Or perhaps it's just that life is back in balance, the life inside my head and heart.

And Mark and I are becoming close friends. Why Mark? Because he's very interesting, interested, spirited, goofy like Joey, adventurous like Nathan *isn't*. And it's just a feeling. He's a sweet soul and a strong soul. I knew it right away when we talked for so long by the window on the train up to Beijing. We will keep this at a good friendship level. Cannot let it go further.

September 16, 1982

Party tonight for Carol.

We danced the hour away to the Beatles, Blondie, on and on. Fame. The Americans in China.

Chinese beer, chocolates, and cake. Smiling faces.

Pleasant summer nights. At one point, Carol and I were dancing and I thought of Cath. Got a letter from her today. I wish she were here.

But these comrades are great.

Good dancing.

We went dancing wild and it felt good. Far away from home, we still carry the spirit with us. Through the dust, the diarrhea, the boards for beds, the thrill of studying here with our Chinese comrades, talking to them. Studying in rooms with cement floors.

Frustration. Everywhere we go we're stared at.

China around us, between us, before us, behind us. Overwhelmed.

We danced to the Beatles and felt a bit of home again. Glad we came, but glad to recall each other and the spirit of the U.S.A.—as we know it.

September 19, 1982   *Sunday morning*

I have just returned from morning exercise with Yang Yang. I met her when Carol, Dianne, and I joined the Chinese department for basketball. For the past two mornings, she has shown me how to do the sequence of exercises that they all do at quarter after six every morning. I don't understand what she's saying half the time, but it's all right. I think she's been enjoying it as much as I have. Sometimes

I spend more concentration on pronouncing the proper tones of the "One! Two! Three! Four!," than on the exercise pattern!

Yang Yang is from Henan province. A fairly tall girl; probably a model's height in Chinese terms. With a wonderful smile. She lived in the foreign students' dorm last year so she is somewhat accustomed to the Westerners.

We have exercised, jumped rope, and sometimes she runs. My lungs are still not ready to run yet after my bout with bronchitis. We walked back to the dorms that are next to one another. The girls are always arm in arm or holding hands. So naturally she took my hand as we walked towards homeward. How did she feel about holding hands with a Westerner? Is it a risk? Will her friends make comments to her about it? She seemed very much at ease, actually.

I still can't believe I'm here.

I learned a whole bunch of words that I must look up this morning.

Bei Hai park with Dianne was wonderful. When we left the dumpling place after lunch (25 cents for a whole lunch but Christ, do I miss tuna fish and salad!), there were blue skies and it remained so the whole day. Both parks were beautiful and the Chinese seemed to be really enjoying themselves. Apparently Bei Hai is the oldest park in Beijing.

Heard voice of Radio Moscow after a thrilling ride home in Chinese traffic. The announcer was explaining how the U.S. was altering Moscow's proposals when relating them to the American public. Proposals on disarmament. That the U.S. was out to dominate. That if Washington was truly in search of peace, if they accepted Soviet proposals, then the world would enjoy peace and safety once more.

How can this be true? Can it be? It's interesting to hear how the other side feels. But how does Yang Yang feel? And how does the average Soviet citizen feel? What's the real story? And whose story counts?

Sweet Joseph, it's not as clear as we might wish it to be.

September 24, 1982   *Saturday, 1:30 pm*

Just came back from lunch with two seniors from the English department; one a member of the Chinese Communist Party, one not a Party member—a rebel. Shit, I can't write, there are too many people in here.

Now they've left. Good. Discussion was on a range of issues: Chinese youth today: they feel they are in a transition period. Confucius is still present, but not as it used to be. They cannot go back. The Cultural Revolution, from 1966-1976, was a gap, a period of time few would like to see repeated. Where to go now? Outside influences are more accessible; attractions present themselves in the Western way of life, free choice, free love, on and on. But the Chinese youth severely criticize the method in which American youth avoid their responsibilities for taking care of their aged parents. They feel this is wrong. They soon will see the trade-offs that come with individualism and freedom.

Divorce is becoming more prevalent.

Unemployment on the rise.

Shakespeare: They love it. But only they have time to read things like this. The worker—and most of China, they claim—does not have time to think on Shakespeare or nuclear war or such things. It is still simply a day-to-day project to survive, for most people.

Hamlet. Othello. A boon to them with its open examination of love, affairs, and jealousy.

Communism v. capitalism: Do you believe in communism? Do you believe in capitalism?

The nature of human beings was a good place to start on that subject. Selfish nature. Survival instinct. We all agreed. But communism, the Party member claimed, was a good way to control this nature, to keep people fed, with a job and in equal relationship with one another. Communism allocates resources equally. And yet a planned economy, it is now clear, does not always dictate the proper path. This, he said, is changing now. More natural forces must be allowed to play. But how does this work?

I explained supply and demand and natural market forces, the benefits of allocation of resources and increasing standards of living, and so on. But the inequities of capitalism, a fact of life in the American system—this I also explained.

"So which do you like better?" they asked. I could not choose. I could only say that from my perspective I prefer to be able to choose my own job, to make decisions like this and others without government influence (at least not direct government influence).

The rebel agreed, he could not choose. "Man, as a part of nature, is not made equal. There are the strong and the weak," he said.

"There is the sun, the ground, the trees, the birds, the tigers. Nature's family is not made up of members that are equal."....?

But they must be given equal opportunity. Inequities in wealth, in opportunity, and therefore inequities in freedom of choice, are a frustrating, even hateful, reality in our system.

Nuclear war? The Soviets?

They said, America does not like the Soviet Union because one strong man does not like another strong man.

"Will you become better friends in the future?" I asked.

Yes, they said.

"We must. They are right on our border. But, it is very hard to trust them." The rebel spoke up, saying that as afraid as they are of the Soviets, they are afraid of the Japanese.

They said to me, no one wants war. No one anywhere wants war. And so we must, all three of us, get along.

That is what I am hoping, I told them.

But China has so little nuclear power, they tell me, as if to say, "Why would we, China, be such a good partner?"

Arms are not the deciding factor, I explained; trust is.

These boys are being trained to be English teachers. Their salaries will be small: an effect of the persecution of intellectuals left over from the Cultural Revolution and in fact prevalent throughout much of Chinese history. The rebel explained to me, however, that the Party member will get a higher job and a higher salary since he is a member of the Chinese Communist Party.

Welcome to China.

September 27, 1982

Spent a few hours after dinner tonight chatting with our new Chinese roommates. One fairly quiet, but friendly. The other, Lin Yi, the one who lives in our room, spirited but polite. Her father is a cadre. I'm not sure why she came to live with us, whether she was picked or whether she volunteered, but she seems to be enjoying herself.

She's very neat.

"We like to go out during the day, not at night," she says.

She admits China is a *developing country* (she found it on my new words list), but is quick to point out that these past few years have brought great progress. I launch into my speech on the amazing change, progress, and potential of China.

This week she has no classes. They work, doing labor—manual labor on campus, the grounds, digging, etc. I was riding home from the Friendship Hotel at three-thirty today, I came upon her, her classmates, and their professor working—digging a ditch. I felt ashamed for some reason to be going to school and not working as they do. I hope they will let me join them.

Discussion of U.S. politics.

Reagan, what do I think of him, they ask. After I finish explaining how I feel, I look at their faces. They are proud of their country. They have gone through terrible times, but things are better now and they are proud of their country. I, however am not proud of mine.

Support of Marcos.

Inconsistent policy toward the Soviets.

A swollen military budget while the poor in our country go starving and homeless.

I suddenly want to have a leader I can be proud of.

It's only now that I realize how sad it is not to believe in my own leaders. Maybe I should be President. And if I were? Would the realities of the situation, the force of circumstance bind me into policies that are wrong, inconsistent, and immoral? There can be no perfection at the top—or anywhere else for that matter. Why can't I accept that? The best place to study a language is in the home country, we discuss. So, you can come to the U.S., and live with me and learn English!

"We are not allowed," they remind me.

"In a few years it will be better," I tell them. Our countries will trust each other more, then it will be easier for you to come.

"I don't think so," Lin Yi says quietly.

Crazy world.

I had a whole afternoon and evening to review words, finally to drill them in. And what did I do? I mailed off the letters on tape to Mom and Dad which included a beautiful bicycle ride and wandering around the haven of the Friendship Hotel. Then, hours talking with my new roommates.

October 2, 1982   *7:30 am, after a somewhat restless sleep*

The night of September 30, Dianne, Xiao Ming, Yin Zi, Alex,

and I met my roommate, Lin Yi, at Tian An Men Square at about half past seven. The ride there was the usual ride down the main drag—I love it. But on this night, all the red flags lined the streets, big round red lanterns adorned every storefront, and people were especially happy and excited (Dianne is snoring as I write). This was the eve marking China's thirty-third year of independence. The country knows how far it has come, it knows the people's potential, and it is excited and proud. Certainly, there are disillusioned Chinese who are not so joyous on this occasion. Amy's new friend, for example—a Chinese rebel who is attracted by American government ideology, economic ideology, "the freedom to choose" (or as Mark and I discussed, the professed freedom to choose).

Amy's rebel friend hates Mao Ze Dong through and through, and curses his own life in China, screaming to break away. But many of the Chinese I met seemed sincerely excited on this occasion. Turning down the road that leads to Tian An Men Square, we could see the bright lights, the buildings outlined in glowing white bulbs, red flags flying, and thousands of people. It was a magnificent scene. I can't wait to return tonight.

Our Chinese friends led us to the place where we were to meet Lin Yi. Smiles and grasping of hands. "Welcome," she said. "Look at all the people. Isn't it wonderful?" It was wonderful. We wandered about, talking and such until we got to the Mao memorial end. "Old Heroes Never Die" was engraved with gold writing in marble.

Hero, I thought to myself. Is Mao really their hero? For some, I'm sure he is. I asked Lin Yi and Cai Jie who their heroes were. Both replied with the name of a Russian novelist. Who was my hero, they asked.

My father, I replied.

We sat and ate mooncakes that Dianne and I brought, and looked at the moon, as one is supposed to do on the moon festival holiday that fell on the same day as Independence this year.

Yes, I could see my loved ones far away on the face of the moon. I thought of Mom and Dad, whose picture I keep by my bed, the one of them sitting on the truck at the ranch. I do miss them—more than I ever have. I guess it's because I don't know when I'm coming home. A year won't be enough here. I can tell I will stay here for two years or be sorry I left too soon. In one year I can learn to communicate; the second year, I can *do* the communicating. I think of Joe and Peter and Sal, I think of Tony at Tufts, and my morning runs down the Green Bay trail. Sometimes I think of Nathan—but not so much these days. I do miss my family, my boys, my sweet daddy, and my dynamic mother. Oh well, perhaps they'll come here to visit.

Now where was I? Well, I got some good people pictures at Tian An Men Square. At certain points crowds gathered around us. My Chinese friends know I hate it and that I find it embarrassing and an invasion of privacy. Each time the crowds circled us, they took my hand and we walked away. They are very sensitive. They love touching my hair and are constantly playing with it. It's cute. It reminds me of me, touching a good friend's hair as I talk to her. They remind me of me in many ways. More on that later; it's too self-centered a topic for me to tolerate at this point.

They are wonderful hosts, as usual. At about quarter past nine, Dianne and I left to go to a party that turned out to be out in hell and gone. We rode for an hour searching for it. And it was cold out. There we were, riding down a nearly deserted highway at speeds that were almost frightening to me. Yes, we felt free. There we were in China! Flying down the highway, exploring a new area. It was the eve of Independence Day in a developing country: an incredible feeling, and we were off to dance. How we miss dancing.

At the party I met a young Chinese man, Jin Hui, a boy—a man-child. I was impressed by his command of English and by his beautiful face. We chatted and I learned that he did not make high enough scores to get into a university. He wished he could have gone. Christ, my blood boils. Ironically enough, I also learned in that conversation that he had taught himself English from the TV and the radio.

"Do you like your job?" I asked.

"Not really," he confided in me. "I would rather go to school."

Maybe it was just part of him, but he lacked the fear that I have felt from many Chinese when they talked to me.

I knew I wanted to see him again. He disappeared into the crowd. I danced and chatted till one-thirty in the morning. Tired of the crowd, I walked over to a secluded area and sat down. There I took a napkin and wrote down my name and address and a note to please call. I was talking to Harry when Dianne came up. "We're going to leave soon," she said. My Chinese friend had already gone. I had to get the note to him. Harry said, "Go for it! I'm right behind you all the way." It was crazy but sweet.

I walked outside but I saw no one.

Suddenly he appeared, and I smiled. I saw no one else around. So I handed him the note. At that moment a stranger stopped about two feet away from us and I froze. "Please excuse me," I said, and I began to walk away.

But he said, "Don't worry," and smiled. Something made me stay.

Jin Hui was delighted and asked me to come to Tian An Men Square Saturday evening to see the lights. He asked me if I would call him. But no phone calls were necessary, and it was too dangerous, anyway. We planned when to meet. My American comrades called to me. He shook my hand and I left. Mission accomplished.

We rode home at two in the morning through the empty streets. They were shining, having just been soaked and swept by the street cleaner. It was like a movie. We joked and laughed as we whizzed along through the night.

Back at the dorm—finally. I was exhausted after an hour-long ride. The gates were locked as we expected. We went to the wall behind the foreign student's dorm and climbed over. Scary as hell. The guys were strong and helped us, as well as our bicycles, over the wall. We climbed in through a bathroom window. Home at last.

I could only sleep until nine o'clock. It was Independence Day. Dianne watched me in amazement as I got dressed and prepared to go to the park. I had a lovely ride. The sidewalks were a sea of colors —everyone was wearing traditional clothes today, compared to the usual workday. Bright reds and oranges and all that. A man walked up to me inside the park—twenty-five—an engineer. He graciously showed me through the park.

After high school he had suffered through two years of hard labor, then off to college. Mao—a good man turned bad, he explained. It was a terrible waste of time, he said.

He took me to a park restaurant to eat. By that time I was exhausted. We took pictures of each other and I went home, flopped into bed. At about quarter till five, Dianne came into the room and crawled into my bed. We discussed the problem of her growing relationship with Aaron and her boyfriend back home. This wasn't what we came to China for, we both agreed. Damn it.

But I think I cheered her up. Sweet woman. I know she'll be all right.

The party that the university's foreign office gave for us that night was amazing. Fifteen tables decked out with fruit and sweet cakes and nuts. All the lights were on, and there were streamers everywhere. Singing from the Japanese, the Chinese. Then we sang a few American songs—poorly, I might add. I know what an extravagance this party was, and I was warmed by their extension of welcome. Even the president of the school was there.

Fell into bed later that night, happy and content. Dianne just woke up. Hair in all directions, smiling eyes. "I love sleep," she says sighing and stretching a bit.

Time to get some studying done. Did I mention that I called Cath? She sounded good, I think. But pressured, still sort of defensive, but not too bad. We had a wonderful talk. Energy and support across the phone lines. And she's still just as enthusiastic as ever. Sweet spirit! I love her.

October 4, 1982

Studied at the math building classroom where many Chinese students study. Cement floors, dusty rooms. Even so, a young man placed a newspaper on the wooden desk chair before he stepped on it to turn on a light above us. A beetle flew by my nose and I looked up only to see a room dotted with black Chinese hair, heads bent studying. Here is the seed of China's progress.

Speaking of progress...

I went to see the eightieth anniversary school play. Xiao Ming and Yin Zi brought the tickets in the afternoon. They were not allowed up to the room so they called to me from outside below my window. They were excited for us to see the play and now I know why. The main idea of the play was the rising up of the students in 1926. Women students, fighting for freedom in work and love, and freedom to allow communism to thrive. It was the strength of the women rising: one girl left her lover for the cause. Lu Shun, of course, was the hero, though he was portrayed as a Communist, which Phillip tells me he was not. Death and violence in the struggle, struggle, struggle—freedom for which they are still fighting today. Many times I watched only the audience. I watched their faces: some lacking expression, so many eyes glued on the play with a look of empathy and fascination to be watching a bit of their lives on stage.

I was quite affected by the whole thing. I take so many freedoms for granted at home. Freedom to walk with whom I like in the street without fear of being watched. Freedom to hold hands without fear of criticism. Freedom to choose my own job. Freedom of expression. On and on.

It's a turning point, my Chinese friend reminds me. Perhaps now things will change. Who knows?

October 10, 1982   *Sunday evening, 10:30*

Jin Hui.

This was our second secret meeting. We met in the darkness at Tian An Men Square and walked through the Forbidden City. Though he didn't make the top 5 percent to get into college, he studies on his own. His English is much better than my Chinese. We discussed FDR, whom he admires—I gave him the revisionist viewpoint which he found interesting—talked about Israel. Christ, if only we could communicate in a common native language. He wants to travel to foreign countries but can't, of course. This, he says does not make him angry. But he is clearly frustrated by it. And yet he understands the reasons for restrictions on freedom of job choice, etc. His acceptance, almost passivity at times, seems common among the Chinese—except for a few. Even Yang Yang will not rise up and cry out. She only boils inside and squeezes my hand as we walk through the park.

"Spirit," he says. "This is most important. Spirit and love between men and women."

Still, he frequently asks how much things cost back home, delighted and amazed by the differences between China's economy and that of the U.S.

Tonight, after exchanging two letters during the week, we met at the bus stop across the street from the school. To Bei Hai park we went.

Words, new words, shared more pictures—one of which he gave me. Beautiful man-child. Looking up a word in the dictionary. Both of us crouched over the book, his hand touched mine, carefully, tenderly. I lost my concentration and struggled to remember the word I was looking for.

We had yogurt and pastry across the street from the park. Here I learned that his family would worry if they knew we were seeing each other. He worries about the government. I worry, too. His letters to me arrive torn open and inspected. But we have spent such wonderful times these past two meetings. It's not only a valuable insight into Chinese young people, but he is special and calm, quiet, happy, alive, and sensitive.

We stood by the lake at the railing and looked out over the lily pads. Here I learned the words for *stars*, "like the light in a girls eyes," he told me and smiled. A warm, firm hand grasped mine, holding my two hands in his gentle, sweet. We talked on and on.

"I'm leaving in two years" I recalled aloud.

"I know," he said. "Maybe you will stay longer...."

Maybe we will have to say goodbye. At this point, that seems eons away.

Dear Daddy, he is treating me the way I have always wanted to be treated. With attention, care, slowly and gently, sincerely.

Why did I allow this to begin? I don't know, but it's fascinating and wonderful. It's nothing like courtship in the States. Jin Hui and I will never sleep together. It's wonderful. The blooming relationship revolves around an entirely different world.

I came back and Lin Yi questioned me. I was a bit nervous. Damn it, why can't my acting hold up at this crucial point? I don't trust her.

Sweet man-child, welcome to a new adventure. You can be sure I will treat you well.

Is this my life? I'm living a dream. I told him tonight.

Where are you, Nathan?

October 11, 1982

I listened to myself as I told Lin Yi and Cai Jie about the States tonight. Rape. Cost of higher education, people's "Me #1" attitude instead of unity, the treatment of minorities.

"Why not live in China?" I find myself wondering. Then I sit down at the desk. Everyone is gone from the room. I glance at the picture of Jin Hui. Spirit. "Why not live in China," I wonder.

Then I recall the letter I wrote to Joey. I feel the flood of Yang Yang's blood as it boils over in fury about lack of choice of lifetime occupation after graduation. I think of Jin Hui's frustration about being unable to travel abroad because the government won't let him leave the country. I look at the picture of my dynamic though crazy, loving family—the picture that sits here on my desk—and I remember why I could never live the rest of my days in China.

12:30 am

Yes, this too is a peaceful time of day. Silent.

A letter from Tom and Deb today. Is what I'm doing so special as they say? Some days I take it for granted.

Back in the U.S., Cathy is probably eating lunch at Fletcher right now. Perhaps Beth is eating at Dewick. Jin Hui is practicing his calligraphy. Daddy's having lunch, looking out at the back yard.

What is Brian doing?

I'm going to sleep.

But I'm not tired.

Lin Yi was angry at Reagan today. She stared at the ground and spoke of Taiwan, seemingly cursing Reagan and his policies that trespassed on China's domestic issues.

Do Chinese people look at me on the street in view of Reagan's policies on Taiwan? I'm still out of touch with so many of the colors, the hues that paint the changing reality of existence here.

October 20, 1982

Yes, the same internal struggles are still with me. One part of me so secure, the other part much too sensitive and vulnerable. How to reconcile these raging, clashing personalities within me? My Chinese still being at an uncomfortably low level compared to what I wish it was, the insecure Basha is surfacing this week, driving me (and my roommate) up a wall. I'm just trying to live through it. But I've got to drink less coffee and learn to take people less seriously. The happy medium is hard to find.

Jin Hui called tonight to make plans for the weekend. A few nights ago I received his letter when I got home. Where is this going? How could it be happening? How can I let it happen? He thinks he knows me, but he really does not. And I, likewise, do not know him. The language barrier is still a significant factor. And yet, we struggle along, conversations filled with dictionaries and rough translations.

Sweet boy. He doesn't even know who he's falling for. Perhaps it's America that he's infatuated with and not me. He loves it here, he tells me, even though we've thoroughly discussed the things he's discontented with. And is it perhaps China that I'm infatuated with and not him? I refuse to belittle our feelings this way.

An early morning riser he is! Up early to practice calligraphy. It is a clear, peaceful time of day, he tells me. Ah yes, my boy, you are one of my kind. Recall riding down back streets of Beijing at eleven at night singing "Joe Hill" and "Edelweiss."

Professor Dong gave tutoring tonight. "We are one country," he tells me of Taiwan and China. "We think the same. In ten years, we will be unified," he says looking at me closely.

"But your ecomonic systems are not the same," I say.

"No matter," he says. "They can live side by side."

Under one government? No way. I love Professor Dong's class. He is dynamite. It makes me want to teach.

Letter from brother Peter today. Reminiscences of our family trip to Europe in 1976, talk of the band, his music, his rapport with Rob, his approach to challenges, and how he feels we are fit to handle our struggles. We are. "I'm sleepy, but I needed to talk to you," he wrote. Sweet brother, I love you so. And a picture sketched at the bottom of the letter, of a farm nestled in the mountains. I want to stay here in China forever. And yet, when I think of the U.S., and all it has to offer—so much opportunity and my family there as well—I know I will return home.

I only hope that by that time I will have learned to reconcile these two extreme parts of me. The strong super woman and the overly sensitive girl. They're killing me this week. Must learn to re-lax a bit more. Not to care less, but to cool out a bit.

During the visit to the town of Cheng De, Professor Shu really gave me his best. Where's the bitterness in him from the Cultural Revolution? Nowhere to be found. Only a strong body and spirit. His dynamism was catching. We talked until one in the morning. I could have stayed all night, even if he is forty-nine years old. I'm a sucker for a brilliant, spirited man with a beautiful smile.

Must sleep. It's half past midnight.

Not tired, but I must sleep!

Back in Beijing

At the top of the mountain with Jin Hui, we took a few pictures. They will be treasures. Then we found a quiet spot to have lunch. He had packed a beautiful picnic lunch of ham and tomato sandwiches, ginger ale, beer, napkins, real bread. Even a table cloth. Sweet man-child. Even talked and read through part of the Declaration of Independence and Kennedy's American University speech. Then we looked again at my pictures from home.

I cannot recount the rest. I was looking at a picture, I don't remember which, when he kissed me on the cheek. The first kiss. Sweet nuzzle into my warm cheek. I smiled. A kiss and another and we were in each other's arms. I would have made love to him had I had my diaphragm. He gasped when he first saw my breasts. Just like a little boy. I felt funny about it—as if I were robbing the cradle. We sat there and talked and loved until three or so. Kisses and searching in the dictionary intermingled as we lay there on the mountainside.

It was time to be clear. He professed love—I told him he didn't yet know me and I didn't really know him. Finally, I know love takes a long time to cultivate.

"It's true," he said. "But feelings can become very strong in a short time," he explained. This is his first love. Help!

I don't know who I will marry, when I will marry, what my life will be, I told him. Now he knows. I wonder if he understands.

Even so, the idea of returning to America came back into the conversation. Perhaps I will come, too, he said. What could you do there to make a living, Jin Hui? It's not easy in America—especially if you don't have a college education. Why did it have to be Jin Hui? His future—not the kind of prospects I dream of.

But then I think of this scene: climbing down the mountain together. Onto the bus: the sun setting, it is very crowded in the bus. We are squashed up next to one another. One pair of hands finds the other and holds tight.

He is tired after a fierce orgasm in my hands, but happy, and as we go along he quietly sings into my ear "Edelweiss," a song from Korea, a love song from the Soviet Union, and a song from Argentina. Beautiful voice. He kisses me tenderly on the forehead when no one is looking. It is too dark to see anything.

"Do you think I can make you happy, Basha?" he asks me.

Yes, I think he could. It's still so easy to fall back into the "Love Is Enough" syndrome. But you know, perhaps it *is* when it's real. But what is real love? The eternal question.

I've never met any man like him before. Of course not.

Political situation here: terrible.

Solution: leave.

Yet, he's very nationalistic about the Han clan. Good people.

Holding hands. He looks down at our two hands and says, "Chinese hand, American hand, together. It's beautiful."

And it is! But can we live forever on that? Spirit. Endurance. Childlike caring and sensitivity. These things we share in common. Yet he knows a life I do not know.

"Perhaps I could live here," I mention. Perhaps.

How many lives I could have. Which to choose? Or which will be chosen for me?

Lin Yi sits next to me studying. During break today, I met my new friend who is an English teacher here. Every Friday she has political study. Workers, students, everyone has it once a week, she explains.

Soon I will call my brother Joseph. He said to call collect. I miss him. Soon I will call. But first I have to buy a winter jacket before I can ride downtown again at night.

The Chinese girls at lunch today were a riot. Lin Yi is different from them. I can't quite figure it out. Haven't seen Yang Yang in days. I wonder where she is?

Must do some characters. Spero, be careful. Don't fuck up your life. Remember your goals.

What are they?

October 26, 1982

Today I have my head screwed on a bit better. Away from Jin Hui's smile, his touch, I think a bit more clearly, a bit more objectively. I'm not going to sleep with him. To him that would mean a lifetime commitment, which in the clear light of day, by myself, I realize that I don't want to give.

This love affair must be cooled down to a friendship. Yes, I think of his devotion, sincerity, how much he respects me—and I am tempted. But recall, Basha, as important as those things are, there are other things, too. Christ, I feel so cold and calculating, but damn it—I can't help but think.

I picture me, sitting on the porch with Daddy, discussing the whole thing. Think of tomorrow, too, he would say. As crucial as it is to live for today, one must also consider tomorrow sometimes. He has no college education. What would he do in the States? What would the two of you do in China? If it were another man, it might be different.

Thanks, Daddy. I love you so for always being with me, helping me to see things clearly. But most of all, it is my decision.

I also realize that the political situation and the pressure it creates has made it impossible for Jin Hui and I to continue. The Foreign Student's Office, a group of Chinese professors and administrators who watch over the foreign students, has been opening the letters and poetry Jin Hui has been sending me through the mail. Finally, last week I was warned that my friendship with Jin Hui was not a "good thing." I was told that if we continued to see each other, he would find himself in trouble.

I see no way out but goodbye.

October 27, 1982

No time to finish that entry. And must go off to class now. Jin Hui will get the letter today. My decision is made. Sweet boy. I'm so sorry.
Crazy world.

The realization of the political situation here has aged me ten years in the past few days.

November 2, 1982

Well, that episode has come and gone. One might say, well, Jin Hui has to live with it; at least I can go home. But he had shared his soul with me and we have shared our love. And so he has become a part of my heart's land. I may return home; of course, I *will* return home, but I will always recall this man-child and his situation here. He is just one in a billion who suffer from this social and political oppression. Thanksgiving is coming. Now I know what to be thankful for: for my freedom. But now that the situation here in China has touched me personally—literally torn a love from my arms— something inside of me will never be the same. At first sad, later with hope and joy, I will remember Jin Hui.

November 6, 1982

I am sitting at the desk practicing Chinese characters. Lin Yi is at the typewriter. A fascination to her and Cai Jie who have never used one.

Suddenly I think about why I have trouble taking a stand on particular political and economic issues. The reason in part is because I have trouble reconciling my image of the ideal with my knowledge (or perception) of reality or the *real*, existing situation. I have become accustomed to the realist school of thought, which disregards ideals or utopian ideas simply because they are (or *seem* to be) impossible under the present conditions. And yet, something inside of me still hopes the ideal is possible.

November 8, 1982

Today I read in the *China Daily* that there was a a coup in Upper Volta. I remember helping Sam write his application for the Peace Corps last spring. He was accepted and sent to Upper Volta. I searched through my address book but his address in Africa was nowhere to be found. The paper says the country has been sealed off (transportation, communication, etc.). What a fucking crazy world we live in. And we, the privileged children of the bourgeoisie, bored with comfort and luxury, ship ourselves off to these hot spots that are ready to burst. Our lives too humdrum, so we must live in danger and in the unknown to provide excitement and a sense of challenge.

I know why Sam went to Upper Volta. He wanted to do something worthwhile. He wasn't quite dynamic and aggressive enough to be able to show his worth in the Tufts atmosphere where people are judged on the basis of sophistication and brilliance, instead of compassion for humanity. So he went to a place where they appreciate his compassion, where he can be appreciated for his strengths and not condemned for his inability to act like a suave eastern academician.

But I didn't even imagine in my wildest of dreams that November would bring a coup to Upper Volta and Sam would be sealed off from the rest of the world.

I wonder what it was like in the few days before the coup? Did people know it would happen? And what is it like now? What are the people there saying about it? I'm dying to know. But I lost his address.

Damn.

November 9, 1982

When I walked out into the hall during break time today, a few of my Chinese girlfriends came over and handed me the words to "Blowin' in the Wind." They wanted to sing. Ruo-xin also came over and listened to us sing. Sweet boy.

I'm finding it easier to make friends among the Chinese now. I met Ruo-xin during break time a week ago. He was standing in the hallway chatting with Dianne. I walked over and introduced myself. He met me with a warm and confident smile. So many friendly people here.

Anyway, just by chance, I bumped into him as I was walking down the steps after class that day. He was almost too embarrassed to talk to me, but he couldn't hide for long. The smile lit up his face as we met at the bottom of the stairs. I managed to get him to offer to help me find a winter coat in town on Wednesday. Now at least we'll have a chance to chat without all his classmates standing around staring. Wednesday should be fun—if we can only take the silly grins off our faces when we see each other.

"How many years must some people exist before they're allowed to be free . . .," we sang. I looked at their faces. If only they were *really* free, then what would their lives be, what would their education be, what would their working years be? I looked at Ruo-xin and wished I could take him home with me. Wished he had been born American. But then, we all had to go back to class (I loved Dong's class today, as usual). As Ruo-xin and his buddy walked arm in arm back to their classroom, a friend came up behind them and hopped on their backs. They all laughed, putting their arms around each other. They are happy here, in many ways they're very happy. But it's not enough. As they get to know the outside world better, will they long for more freedom? Or will they be content with China as she is (as she is raising her standard of living, etc.), simply because it is— and now I realize this is no small factor—their homeland?

November 10, 1982

The wind came down from Siberia yesterday. Huge gusts of cold air put color in our cheeks but sent me running home to crawl under the covers to drink hot milk for lunch. Yum! But didn't stay cozy for too long as I had to meet a friend at half past one to go into town. We wanted to go browsing through bookstores. I was looking for a particular book, but we never found it.

No great loss, the day was wonderful anyway. Ruo-xin took me to an area downtown behind Tian An Men Square that is teeming with

"Young People's" shops—shops that are privately owned. We wandered down the narrow streets and stared at all the people. Then I bought my winter coat. Bright red. At around four o'clock we began to get hungry so I suggested we go back to school in time to catch dinner at quarter past five. He thought for a moment and then smiled and said, "Would you mind going to my house first? You could meet my parents" (who are retired and stay at home and take care of their grandson, whose parents work). Well, of course, I was delighted.

We rode over to Wang Fu Jin Street and then turned down a little alley that led to his "house." On the way he explained that like most Chinese, his house was very small—"*too* small," as he put it—and on and on about how inadequate it was. I told him to say no more, that these things weren't very important to me.

The house: House? No. Shack? Yes.

He ducked his head to enter through the low archway (he's rather tall for a Chinese), which led into a muddy pathway, narrow, with cement walls on the side. We passed a few open doors until we came to his family's place.

"This is it!" he said. The roof was thatched with grass growing on it, the usual clothes hanging out to dry by the side of the house, and a small supply of cabbage sitting outside to keep cool. We walked into the first "room," which was actually a tiny porch with a small stove, a table, and two chairs—"the kitchen," he explained. The kitchen? I guess we'd call it a storage room with screens.

"Ba Ba," he called out. "I brought a friend home."

His father came out to the kitchen and looked at me. "Oh, it's the foreigner!" he said, smiling. Introductions and all that. My friend was grinning from ear to ear and so was I; we were really getting a kick out of it—each of us for separate reasons, I'm sure.

The other two rooms were the bedroom, which is also the study and the playroom, I guess, and then a room with a few chairs and a radio and a TV. Everything was very neat, but crowded as hell. It was quite warm inside, and really rather cozy. It's hard to make grey cement walls look cozy, but they had a few maps hanging up and towels acting as drapes over the windows. Still, it was the warm smiles and the honest, attentive manner with which they treated me and their son that made the place seem like a mansion. His mother was in the sitting room, reading—a lady about sixty-five years old who immediately handed me a glass of tea and the most comfortable chair in the room. She asked me whether Nixon was still President, and I told her with a straight face, "No, we have President Reagan now." What a riot. I suddenly realized that not everyone in the world keeps up with political events!

I didn't feel I knew them well enough to ask too many questions, so I just answered theirs. Later his mother disappeared into the kitchen, refusing our offer to help her make dinner. We sat and read the paper together, I fumbled along. The newspaper is still really hard to understand. Listened to a cassette of foreign movie themes. It has been banned since its publication two years ago, but they still listen to it in this household.

Before we knew it, dinner came out. My favorite, *jau dz* (steamed dumplings). We dipped them, steaming hot, into vinegar and soy sauce, drank tea, and had tiny little oranges for dessert. I was stuffed. His parents insisted we eat, just the two of us, and they came in and out to watch us eat and to make sure we had enough. It was really cute.

Finally we had to leave; it was already dark and we both had a lot of homework to do back at school. His brother, who works on the western border of China in a chemical factory and was home for a visit, walked us to the end of the lane and we said goodbye. As we rode down Beijing's main drag I looked over at my friend. Now I know him a bit better. On Sundays he goes home, they make dumplings, sit around, eat, and talk in that little sitting room. I wish I could express more clearly what the house felt like. And what I felt like sitting there, "The foreigner who came to dinner."

November 11, 1982   *(actually 1:00 am, November 12)*

Got my period two weeks early. That's a new one for me!

This morning I sat in on a lecture, "Socialism and the Unemployment Problem." My friend, Sun Hua, from the economics department, invited me to come. Well, there we were, sitting there waiting for class to start. In walks the professor. He walked out amongst the students and chatted, then came over to me to find out who this new face was and how I got in. I wanted to say, "Well, I'm a flaming running-dog capitalist but I want to hear you lecture, just to hear how the other side thinks." But instead, my friend spoke up (for a girl with a tiny frame, she's even got more spirit and gumption than I do). Explained who I was and all that. The professor smiled and asked me how I was feeling, had I "adjusted" yet (the Chinese favorite question to ask foreigners), and he'd try to speak a bit more slowly during lecture for my sake.

My economics vocabulary is very small, but growing now that I've made friends with Sun Hua and her roommates. I caught a few words here and there (planning, incentives, bonus, socialism), and Sun Hua kept her hand on the dictionary the whole hour and a half, searching for the words she knew I didn't understand. This afternoon we're going to go through her notes slowly together—then I'll really know what I heard this morning. She's a pretty nifty lady.

The next day: Well, wouldn't you know it. I met Sun Hua at dinner last night and she pulled me aside with a weird look on her face. The gist of her message was that after the economics class yesterday, the prof talked to her privately. He said, "You can't bring your American friend to this class anymore. There are certain things we discuss in here that foreigners are not yet allowed to know." She was so embarrassed to have to tell me that I couldn't come anymore. There I had sat in that classroom, eyes fixed on the professor, and felt quite at home. Why not? It's education! And education is free, open, and for everyone to enjoy if they so choose.... Not so in China.

Well there's a shocker. Something I thought was a *given*, a basic fact, a natural right, is *not*. There I was with my Western concept of freedom of education shining in my eyes, wandering into a Chinese classroom thinking I could listen to any class I wanted to. Naive.

"It's not that way in China," she said to me. "Freedom and education don't live in the same house." Now I realize what a special right it is to study what we please, be able to listen to any class, or use the resources of our library freely. It's amazing.

So, Thanksgiving is here. I have been here only two and a half months and already I realize what I have to be thankful for back home.

Freedom, a society, a way of life (all of which have their good points and their bad points), which I had begun to take quite for granted. We are so lucky to live in America. It's nice to finally feel proud of my homeland. (Not to say that we aren't screwing up as we deal with our internal problems as well as our relations with the rest of the world, which is looking more dismal everyday.)

I wish I could be with my family on Thanksgiving. I certainly will be thinking of them.

I am thankful for the chance to live here, to get to know this interesting and often startling country. I am thankful for the new perspective. That perhaps has been the most amazing part of this experience—the growth of a new perspective on my life, the life of other people around the world, and our relationship.

But most of all, I am thankful that on cold days I can turn my head to thoughts of you, my family, to know that you are happy and healthy. I am thankful for your support in my adventures. And I am thankful that many months from now, when I return home, we will be able to share our thoughts and our love.

Those are my Thanksgiving thoughts. Though haphazardly written, I think you all get the message.

Ruo-xin's room today. Really not as crowded as other rooms I'd been in. He was out of the room when I arrived, so I stood and waited for him. He came in, a smile lit his face. What a cutie. But I'm having progressively more trouble understanding his Chinese—today especially. He's speaking as if he were talking to a native sometimes, and I just don't understand. It's so frustrating. Normally, in "this kind of situation," I could be so talkative, ask questions, on and on. But today I simply waited for him to raise each topic, I stumbled along and only hoped he would understand. I just don't want him to get bored with me.

Now I'm being silly. Go back to sleep, Spero (where I've been since nine this evening—I was exhausted from this forty-year day).

November 12, 1982

My half birthday today.

"So, what have you got to say for the first half of your twenty-first year?"

Hmmm...

All I can say is, it's dusk right now. Actually, almost dark. Beautiful. The shadows of Beijing's buildings are the only things I can see outside, besides dark figures peddling bicycles along the street. The lamplight is warm and soft yellow. I feel relaxed and content after a tender interlude between the sheets with Mark. His body was strong and heavy on top of mine. Each thrust, so long and slow, drew the loneliness out of my heart. Just to hold someone feels so good. And I get such a kick when a friend can be a lover, too. James Taylor crooning away. I think of Nathan, of Cath, of my two brothers, sweet Sal,

Mom and Dad. Here I am, finally, in China. That's what I've got to say. Right now, I couldn't ask for more.

Don't worry Cary, I haven't left my "Westernness" behind, I haven't rejected it. I'm only experimenting with another perspective.

But this afternoon. I was home again for a while.

November 13, 1982   *Saturday afternoon*

That was a sweet night. Mark and I sat in the vacant Friendship Hotel dining room and ate dinner. Tall ceilings, looks like a movie set. We drank beer, smoked cigarettes, and covered the spectrum of our thoughts. Very thoughtful guy. I guess the first genius I've ever known besides Uncle Marty. But what a confused head. Happiness once again proved inversely proportional to intelligence. But together we had a good time. Took a taxi home! Such a decadent day. Walking down the tree-lined lane of the university, we held hands and thought about the words of the evening. I slept well.

Today I awoke around seven o'clock and worked on some of my "outside-of-class" words.

In the afternoon I bought some oranges and walked over to Ruo-xin's room. He was so glad to see me, as I was to see him.

To live in the mountains where it's peaceful: Campful. Taiwan. Physics. Smiles. The ever-present dictionary.

We sat on his bed, ate oranges, and whispered while his room-mates slept.

Enough fun and sweet afternoons.

Now to study!

November 19, 1982

Another week has whipped by.

My chinese is still on the plateau—ugh!

Did everything but study this week. Went to the zoo with Ruo-xin, called Mom and Dad for Thanksgiving, went to the Forbidden City with Yang Yang, stayed up late and talked to Chen Long, de-cided to go to Inner Mongolia for Thanksgiving, skipped class on Thursday. Conversation class is really slowing down to a snail's pace and it's driving me up a tree—so I'm trying to ignore it. Spent an afternoon with Sun Hua, who has taken on the crusade of trying to perfect my Chinese tones.

The lights were out all over campus when Yang Yang and I got back last night at six. I could see the stars so clearly. It almost looked like Montana. We sat around with candles, Lin Yi, Cai Jie, and I (Dianne was out with Aaron) and chatted a while. I went later to get water and made a detour to Mark's room—actually, he heard me cursing as I tried to go down the cement stairs without breaking my neck; I couldn't see a thing. I went in and found him standing in the middle of the dark room.

"Fun, huh?" I said smiling.

"Yeah, a riot," he said in a teasingly sarcastic tone.

"I can smell you a mile away," I told him truthfully. He has a unique scent.

"Now here's some intimacy, just handed to us. A dark room and we didn't even have to turn the lights off," he whispered.

No one in the hall. No one else in the room. No one else in the world, for just that moment. I kissed him and smiled.

"I'm going to get water," I said. "See you later." I must try to keep my distance.

I was exhausted. Absolutely drained. So I fell asleep at about quarter after eight, just woke up now at about half past twelve. Dianne had come home and a book called *Photographing America* had come in the mail. It's amazing. They'll flip when they see what my country looks like. Even I flipped. It's funny what you take for granted when you see something so often. I realize how spectacular the whole place is, now that I've seen something different.

November 20, 1982

Hmmmmm.

Haven't been plastered in months. Tonight we had a party with the Japanese. Now *they* know how to party! We ate and drank and ate and drank. And then one Japanese guy got up to sing for us. Then another. Sweet love songs. Then it was time for an American to sing. Who else did everyone ask but me, of course. I was so tipsy, so why not? Suddenly the picture of the bomb dropping on Hiroshima flashed before my mind's eye. There was only one song I could sing after that, "Last night I had the strangest dream I'd ever dreamed before. I dreamed the world had all agreed to put an end to war. . . ."

And so it went. I sang my favorite message. Everyone cheered. I sat down and we all drank up another glass in honor of the dream my song spoke of. Here we are, nearly forty years later, sitting together, eating and drinking and singing—after inflicting such horror in World War II. There's hope for us yet.

Recall Phillip and Chris with their imaginary guitars singing a hopping Grateful Dead tune. We laughed so hard. The first time I listened to a Grateful Dead tune and didn't think of my first love, Peter Drew. Sweet Peter Drew. I remember dancing to the Dead with you. Fine memories. Precious love. Special man. I miss you.

November 21, 1982

A grey Sunday morning.

We all reached out last night. The *Americans in China* book, not yet written, was at the top of my thoughts as I went to sleep last night.

Mark puking in the bathroom.

Philosophical discussion as we huddled around the radiator.

Dianne in Aaron's arms listening to jazz and feeling sad.

Dancing in the hall at night.

Reeva's life story in Italy.

Dianne's call says "Come home, Bess." Holding her tight.

"They don't understand us here, or do they?"

Pens from Nathan and a beautiful letter. Silly dreams we have.

Listening to Brian's tape from Boston over again. Another love that leaves sweet memories in my heart.

So many people I want to write.

Getting ready to travel at Thanksgiving.

Many of us traveling alone with mixed feelings. Wanting to be independent but only feeling lonely and scared.

November 24, 1982   *Wednesday morning*

I leave for Inner Mongolia this afternoon. Hard seat. Twelve hours. Should be quite an adventure.

Ruo-xin is sending me off—he insisted. Sweet boy. Walking around campus last night, he wearing his big People's Liberation Army jacket, looking like every other male I see. The stars were so clear. Quite a wind. I wanted to snuggle up against him, but of course, could not. We could only smile. And for now, that is enough.

I'm excited to travel, yet scared. I wish it were already time to get on the train.

(Later.) Recall that lovely morning, the dorm deserted. Crawling into a warm bed with Mark. Cozy and loving. I'll tell you, Spero, you really live.

November 25, 1982
    Inner Mongolia, on the grasslands just outside Huhehaote, the capital.

After a wonderful Mongolian meal of boiled lamb, steamed cabbage, mushrooms, and sweet brandy, of course, I walked back to the yurt with my guide and driver and a Mongolian friend of theirs. A beautiful starlit night here out on the grasslands. Very chilly. Laughing and joking, we left the dining room. Though they live in Inner Mongolia, they all speak Mandarin and my Chinese was in prime form today, so it was a pleasure.

The yurt: a Mongolian-style hut—sort of like a round house, the frame made of bamboo poles covered with animal skins. A hearth in the middle which is glowing almost as much as I am. I made it here by myself, with a little—or I should say a lot—of support and helpfulness from the Chinese people I met along the way. So how did I get here?

Before leaving Beijing, after I finally got out of bed with Mark (who is now in Qing Dao), I went to the travel service to get my train ticket. Packed my back pack. Kissed Dianne goodbye and left Lin Yi sick in bed with a cold. I walked out of the dorm and looked for Ruo-xin's face. I saw him wave to me and so I walked to meet him—and off we went. I must admit I was nervous. Afraid. Scared. Excited. Nothing to say, I was too hyped up inside. Ruo-xin was of course his patient smiling self. Told me to relax, it would be a wonderful trip. "Christ, I hope so," I thought to myself.

Crossing the street to catch the 103 bus, he held my hand for the first time. I squeezed his hand and then he politely let go after we crossed the street. Sweet boy. I'm probably scaring him to death. But by the looks of his smile, I don't think so.

We got to the train station with time to spare. We found my train and the right car. He insisted on taking me inside to help me find my seat. I soon found out why: the car was crammed with frantic, frazzled folks of the Chinese nationality, yapping at the top of their lungs. Ruo-xin's true Han background came through. The words came flowing out of his mouth and he pushed and pulled as they did. We finally found my seat. Everyone in the car was staring at me, the only foreigner in the car. That feeling! Yuk.

"Do you want to come outside for a minute?" Ruo-xin asked me.

"Yes." I really wanted to kiss him right there but that will never happen. One day I will return home to the U.S., and it would only be too sad if we became more than friends. But Christ, it's difficult. He really is wonderful. Enough of that!

So we went outside the car and chatted a bit. Then said goodbye. I was ready to go and he was comfortable enough to say so long. That's a good friend. Wished me a smooth trip and sent me off with a smile. What more could I have asked for?

The train ride was another experience in itself. Riding hard seat from Beijing to Mongolia—thirteen hours in a crowded (three people to a bench), smoky, filthy train car, full of peasants spitting on the floor and toilets that could curl your hair—might sound crazy to the average traveler. But now I know it's the only way to go. Really. There were people on that train from every walk of life. With thirteen hours to share, we (meaning me and the fourteen people in my immediate proximity) discussed the gamut of things from Taiwanese to U.S. lifestyle, to capitalism to Deng Xiao Ping, to the Soviet Union, to food, on and on. It was a priceless experience (and of course was a great workout for my speaking and listening comprehension).

Two cadres, as well as a young girl from Xinjiang, and an old man sat with me. Chatted a bit, the usual questions, and before we knew it, it was dinner time. I of course was allowed to eat only after everyone else was done. I walked into the cold dining car, drank brandy, and ate eggs and rice. Reminded me of the trip up from Canton. The food may have been lousy, the brandy may have been fourth class, but it was heaven to me because I was off on my own to Mongolia, surrounded by Chinese people—the clan I get along with best.

The Xinjiang girl fell asleep in my lap.

The two workers in lambskin coats who sat on the train floor next to my seat revealed in whispers their desire for a capitalist national economy.

Crammed full of people, babies young and old.

The chicken sellers and their antics. Capitalism at work. The men a few seats up eating away at the chicken furiously, like animals. Cleanliness is not next to godliness in this country. I love it!

Then the students came on board. Big heavy coats. We are nearing the really cold spots. Cheeks from the outside got redder.

Christ, the stars are clear tonight.

I arrived in the capital early in the morning, and with the help of a Chinese veterinary school professor I found a hotel. Here they offered a guide and a trip to the grasslands. The price for two days was outrageously expensive, forty American dollars, but the town's maps were all sold out after the summer season (that's socialist planning for you!), so I decided to go for it. What the hell. If I run out of money, I always have my Visa card, right?!!

It turned out to be worth a million bucks. The two-hour drive out to the grasslands was a sight in itself. All the way along, peasants and horses pulling loads of vegetables, wood, animal skins. The countryside was gorgeous even in its desolateness. I think this was because of the people wandering about, talking and laughing as they worked, enjoying a slow-paced existence. Plus the sheep grazing and the Montanalike hills that rose up every now and then.

I spend that night in a Mongolian tent that had a wooden floor, a coal stove, and mountains of blankets to sleep beneath—which I did quite peacefully that night. Woke the next morning to a starlit sky (but the Big Dipper was upside down!) and finally a gorgeous sunrise. It was colder than sin, but I wore four sweaters, long underwear, and my red winter jacket and was perfectly cozy—save my cheeks, which were quite cold. God, it's getting harder and harder to write proper English. Takes much more effort now. I guess when you spend every moment from the time you wake to the time you go to sleep speaking Chinese (I even *dream* in Chinese now—it's a scream!), English slowly slips away and it becomes more and more natural to communicate in Chinese.

That day we (the guide, sweet lady, twenty-seven years old, and a couple from Australia) rode horses to a commune and saw a man skinning a freshly killed lamb. Amazing. I took pictures. Went to a house on the commune. Ate some Mongolian cheese, boiled lamb, steamed dough. Drank Mongolian tea and smoked Mongolian cigarettes (I had to try one, just to see what it was like. *Very* strong, but tasty.) I befriended a Mongolian girl who was walking around outside as we approached the commune. She came into the house with us and we ended up trading songs. The Mongolian songs are gorgeous—a mixture of an Indian scale and a Russian flavor. If only I could imitate it. I sang two songs. My old standby, "Last night I had the strangest dream I'd ever dreamed before. I dreamed the world had all agreed to put an end to war. . . ," on and on. I love that one and I can now give a translation of it before I sing it, so it's double fun! The other song I sang was the one Daddy wrote for Mom when they got engaged, "Morning Rapture." So, you're famous in Mongolia, Daddy. They loved it. Visited a few run-down temples that had been devastated by the Cultural Revolution.

Took an hour nap in the afternoon one day after a tremendous lunch of strangely spiced lamb, mushroom-type soup, beer, and a few unknown-to-me vegetables.

November 26, 1982   *7:00 am*

Woke up at quarter past six, just before the sun began to rise. Clear, fresh air. My fire had gone out and I had to pee, so outside I went. That's why the Mongolians look so tough and healthy. Good, fresh air. The night sky was clear. Too gorgeous to capture in words or a picture. I wandered around outside a bit in awe of the whole scene. A dog barked in the distance.

Warm now, under the many blankets, I sit and think of how much my family would love this morning. It's amazing to experience it alone—it's simple and free and thrilling. But if they were here, it would be even better. Even better? I'm not sure.

While I slept last night, they ate turkey with our cousins, the Shattens. It's still strange to me that I'm not there.

Sweet family, as brother Peter wrote to me, you are more a part of my life than you will ever know. Perhaps that helps make every experience I have so much more wonderful— because I know they are there somewhere, living and loving me.

November 28, 1982

I returned home feeling not only content but victorious. It's a good thing that I came home feeling so wonderful because it helped me survive the blow that came soon after. I received a letter from Cathy the night I got home which said she couldn't decide whether or not to tell me, but since I had been mentioning Nathan so frequently in my letters she decided she had to. A month ago, some old "friends" of Nathan's confided to Cath that Nathan was fooling around behind my back while we were together last year. I could hardly believe it—and I still really can't believe it—and now it really makes very little difference. But all that is too rational. My heart was cut in two and it was all I could do to keep from being severely depressed. I wrote Nathan a letter asking about it. But now that a few days have passed I feel a little less concerned about it. I know my own worth. If someone else doesn't recognize it and has to go off to be with someone else, so be it. As we've already discussed, he's not the man for me, anyway. Moreover, I refuse to spend more than a day wasting time over things like this that I have no control over now.

And before I knew it, my Chinese roommate had come back to the dorm and was knocking at the door, eager to hear the details of the trip.

And what's our motto? "We never give up!" So, instead of dying of a broken heart at the thought of someone I loved and trusted having been unfaithful, I went out and ran a few miles and had dinner.

The moon is almost full tonight. Listening to Jacques Brel, thinking of my teachers and friends, Jackie and Gus. Remembering sitting on the steps of their house talking to Nathan on the phone. Christ, Cathy's letter threw me. I can't believe it could be true. Could it be? Was I so blind? You know, maybe I was.

Ah well, shit. I sent off a letter to him and now I'm not going to kill any more time over it if I can help it. The trip was too exciting, challenging and finally satisfying to let that wonderful feeling slip away, unenjoyed. Men come and go, but the experiences like this trip I must and will treasure down to the last drop.

The girl, singing the Mongolian songs were beautiful—she and the songs. The plain, cement house became a palace when she sang out so clear and strong. The baby played quietly and listened. I tasted Mongolian tea and cigarettes. So much land. What to do with it? They move along, each man and his horse, slowly but surely, happily. What is it that makes them so loving, so cheerful? Is it the clear, star-studded night sky? Is it the fresh, crisp air? Is it the wide, open spaces that my brother Peter loves so much, as does Ruo-xin? Is it the slow pace, time to talk and enjoy, that keeps them smiling?

Still, it was good to get back.

Carol and I have grown closer. It's really quite nice. Wandering through the free market, buying pears and peanuts and chocolate. We've done it, a trip totally by ourselves, triumphant. For some reason we have been able to share our excitement and the bad moments as well. A good woman.

Sat with Ruo-xin tonight and talked about the trip. It was good to see him. He's always got a spare moment to chat, smile, ask a question, walk outside for a while. It's good to be back.

And here in my room, both roommates are out. Solitude. Let my mind rest. After the trip, such a good time and then coming home to a devastating afternoon. I'm exhausted. Sleep, here in China, sleep well, and soundly, and recall, my girl, that the world is yours. You need only live and keep your spirits high, open and free, to enjoy all that is here for you to experience. Don't be afraid of a burn. You know how tough you are now. Live. It's all right.

And sleep well.

December 3, 1982

If only I could freeze time now, I would. Here I sit, in China. In the classroom with one of the biology department groups. They study here every night. Since I've gotten to know Ruo-xin, I have been studying here. He sits beside me doing his physics. Sweet manchild. What would Uncle Dicky say? I think he'd love it. If only he were still alive for me to share it with him.

So there they all sit in green and blue, and a few shades of beige. Some studying, some listening to the volleyball game. Here's a comraderie that doesn't exist back home. Unless I'm getting a false impression. But I don't think so. They hold each other up, love each other, study together, eat together, exercise together. It's very healthy, I think. I love to see it. And even if I can't be a part of it—which I can't (even as Ruo-xin and I grow closer and closer), at least I can sit among it. It warms my soul, my heart, and settles my often troubled mind. The radiator is on, warm. The girl down the aisle smiles at her classmate. Ruo-xin is thinking hard. Back to reading my story in Chinese of the man who lost his horse.

Christ, I hate this journal sometimes! I couldn't possibly express the feelings I have right now. Perhaps it was silly to try to put them down on paper. But I had to try.

What will this China be? What will I be to them years from now?

With all the lack of freedoms here, do I still wish I had been born here? Sometimes.

December 4, 1982   *Saturday, 4:45 pm*

I look out the window and see the sun setting down behind the buildings of Beijing. Sending the sun over to the States where right now they're sleeping peacefully. I miss home today. I miss going to school at Tufts. I feel very unsettled. When will my mind ever be consistently calm? Ever? Never? When? As happy and adjusted as I have become to one way of life, an environment, to one town, I'm always feeling—well, not always feeling, but often missing someone, or some days gone by. Why? It's such an enormous waste of time to dwell on such things.

Three months ago I arrived here. I never knew that being so far away from home would feel this way.

December 6, 1982   *Monday, 9:00 pm*

Christ, what a day this has been. It all began quite normally. I woke up at six o'clock and studied for an hour, drank coffee, and ate a Chinese pastry. Walked to class in the crisp morning air, felt fresh and clean. Took my exam, did OK, I guess. And went out for break. Found Ruo-xin waiting there for me. Sweet boy. Wandered about and talked about our heroes. His, well, he hadn't given it much thought, mentioned two very well-known guys who had saved the lives of so and so in the past few weeks. One guy had plunged into a cess pit to save a guy, one had jumped in front of a train to save a child. Hmmm.

My hero—Daddy. We walked and laughed. Ruo-xin. I enjoy his company. So supportive, so friendly. These people crack me up. Well anyway, on the day goes. I came home from eating yogurt and was listening to the tape from Mom. She's really something else. Such a vigor, and zest. A positive strong spirit. I only hope I can follow her example.

Well, then I was dancing to some disco music on the tape when Reeva came in and said I had a call from the States. Who was it? Sweet Nathan.

"Basha?" he called out. "Are you there?"

"Nathan, my love," I screamed. I couldn't believe he was calling. Right then I knew he had gotten my letter. But not in my wildest dreams had I thought he would call. God, it was good to hear his voice. I miss him so, that pompous ass.

"Is it true, Nathan?" I asked.

"Of course it isn't. Why did you even think twice? Don't you remember what it's like up there at Fletcher?"

"I guess so." Who knows. I guess I'll never really know. But the sound of his voice and the words he spoke (screw him for being such a master of the English language and damn him for knowing just what to say to win my heart) got to me.

"Have you forgotten I love you, Basha?" How could I forget? I love him, too. I always will.

"I couldn't bear to think of you being sad. I talked to your parents last night. We all agreed by the sound of your letters that you're sucking the lemon dry. Are you smiling, Basha? God. I am now."

"I am smiling, Nathan. You are a special man."

He finished writing his thesis. Christmas is coming, he's looking forward to going home.

"I missed hearing your laugh, sweet girl."

On and on. Mongolia. "How's your love life, Nathan?" He laughed.

So she's Catholic, of course. He's known her for two months and now she lets him hold her hand. I felt a twinge, him holding someone else's hand. But then I felt joyous and relieved. I hope we can evolve this love affair into a good lifelong friendship.

"So how's your love life?" he asked me.

I couldn't possibly begin to tell him what's been going on, so I just said there was none.

"I still love you, Nathan." And that's true. That's true. Once I love someone, I never stop loving.

But what was I doing four hours later as the sun was going down? Making love with Mark as the smoke from the coal furnace outside floated into the room. Spero? I blame it all on my promiscuous brothers.

Dianne brought dinner back from the cafeteria. Talked about how our lives were changing this year. We left home for a million reasons. Certain reasons were to escape. She to escape her boyfriend. I to escape my growing boredom, my increasing frustration with my peers. To escape my sheltered existence. To escape those people who can't see further than the nose on their own face. It was the best decision I ever made—to spend my senior year here. With spirited people. Students who share my enthusiasm. And even Americans who I sometimes really like to be with. Other times I can't stand them but I'm sure it's mutual.

And now, well, I ate dinner, got redressed and went off to the classroom. Body and soul alive and warm and happy.

Unfortunately I have cramps with this period, the worst ones I've ever had, that's for sure. Shit, I hope this doesn't become a habit.

I've enjoyed sleeping with Mark, sharing warmth and affection. But I didn't have an orgasm this time. The first time in a long time. I'm not in love with him. So it's not always exactly right. Orgasm doesn't come so easily when you're not in love. Ah, well. It was a nice break, and wonderful to share some affection; I do so miss it sometimes.

So beside me now sits Ruo-xin, memorizing his English book. Literally memorizing. It's crazy, the method of language learning here. But he and his classmates plug along. Sweet smiling eyes. I love the students here. It has renewed my faith in students. But perhaps, as I get a clearer picture of the inside situation—the real situation— I'll feel differently. We'll see. What a day. Craziness. But I feel better than I did two days ago. Yes, that crash was my hormones. God damn it, I could scream!

Cool it, Spero. You'll survive it.

December 7, 1982

Finished my oral midterm. A few of my Chinese friends helped me prepare. All this week, Ruo-xin and his two buddies quizzed me, listened to me bumble through these wonderful Chinese tales. The classroom where I study every night is rather chilly, but Ruo-xin saves me a seat by the radiator. This week, at around ten o'clock, the three of them and I sat around the radiator and went over the fables. I can say it was nothing less than delightful—and I really learned how to tell the tales with style (with a few good colloquial expressions learned along the way). They're great teachers.

I came out of the exam this morning and there they were, waiting to hear how their student had done.

December 8, 1982

It was too uncomfortable.

The girls in Ruo-xin's class/study hall have been giving me cold stares and obnoxious looks and greetings in the hall. Of course I'm oversensitive, but I knew what they were driving at: "What is this girl doing, becoming so close to the guys in our class, particularly to Ruo-xin?" Furious. And inside, they secretly wished they could be that way, too.

But they can't. It's not accepted here.

So I told Ruo-xin I wasn't going to come to the classroom to study anymore, that it was too uncomfortable. He was upset with those girls, explaining that they were extremely closed minded and that the rest of the people liked me to come study there (Christ, my English is going down the drain). Still, I felt sad. Too bad this had to happen. Still, it reinforced the fact that sweet Ruo-xin is a good friend, an understanding friend, an accepting friend. We rode to the northern outskirts of Beijing and chatted, gave a classmate out there a book, and rode back. I sang to him, we talked, and I felt all right— though exhausted, as I've felt for the past four or five days.

Had yogurt when I came back and then dinner. A shower, finally. My body had begun to corrode from all the dirt of four days building up on it without a shower. Studied awhile and then went out to give Ruo-xin some chocolate at the classroom and a note, thanking him for being so understanding. Saw Professor Dong on the way out. He must still think I'm slacking off. Screw you, baby. My classmates are important here, too, not just your lousy class where all we do is memorize.

I felt clean and beautiful and sweet-smelling as I walked through the cool night to the classroom. I hesitated at the door, then walked in. Ruo-xin looked up with that wonderful smile of surprise on his face when he sees me. He was still wearing his People's Liberation Army jacket. I sat down and gave him the chocolate wrapped in blue tissue paper. His hands were warm. My hand rested in his as he held my hand with the package in it. "Just friends, Ruo-xin?" I wondered to myself. I think so. It's all so new to me. A whole new set of social rules, feelings, backgrounds, culture—and yet underneath the same human feelings as I have. When can one cross the line of social habits or social mores for the sake of human feelings? It's hard to know.

Anyway, we chatted awhile. The friend who always wears green came over with a beautiful smile and some questions on English which I answered.

Then the guy from the South came up. Ruo-xin had been talking to him about the whole thing. He usually speaks to me in Chinese, knowing that I want to learn Chinese. But today he broke the rules, wanting to be sure I understood his point.

"Do you miss your family?" he asked.

"Yes, I do. Very much."

Pause.

"Please don't be angry," he said. "It is only a few girls. The rest of us are good. I hope you'll come back here and study with us in our classroom. . . . Those girls don't matter. We like to have you here, to study with you, to talk with you."

I didn't know what to say except thank you. Ruo-xin was glowing and so was I. The room was warm and cozy for once. The Southern friend smiled and then picked up the newspaper to read. I looked around the room. Greens and blues. Padded winter clothing. Heads bent, studying. Here I have found some loving souls. They're all over the world. One just has to be patient and look carefully.

I feel better now. So off to study. Another amazing day in the life and times of this girl from Highland Park.

Highland Park, a town so far away. In another world.

December 12, 1982   *Sunday morning, Cathy's birthday*

We had a wonderful time yesterday. Went to the house and chatted. Before I knew it Ruo-xin's parents had gone into the "kitchen" and we were alone chatting away. How to change China, its government, the job distribution problem. He's a middle-of-the-roader on socialism, just like I am. He appreciates the fact that medical care and education are free. He even thinks relations between people are fairly equal, with very little class difference, which I think is an illusion. It's better than in the States, but it's still an illusion. However, he hates the fact that the government can decide his job for him, that the government decides which classes he takes, that the government decides where he lives. How to explain that you can't have your cake (free education, medical, housing, and low prices) and eat it too (freedom of choice, life style, and so on). We still have so much to say about all this.

"Would you like to go out for a while? Take a walk down Wang Fu Jing Street?"

"I'd love to," I said.

His mother protested, but before she knew it, Ruo-xin had grabbed my hand and we were making our way down the narrow icy lane toward the main street. It was just past dusk, all the lights were on, people were bustling home from work, looking in the windows, buying books, laughing, buying vegetables and meat and sweets for dinner. We walked arm and arm through the street, watching the crowd. Went into a few book shops to look around. Dinner was wonderful, except my stomach started hurting—a stabbing pain in the tract that leads into the stomach or out of it, I'm not sure which. Damn my stomach!

A program from England that teaches English was on television and we watched it intermittently throughout dinner. Ruo-xin and I got pleasantly tipsy. His father is a sparkler. He even said Ruo-xin and I could go traveling together this coming vacation. "I completely agree to it," he said with a broad grin. This is interesting. (Ruo-xin and I couldn't help but nearly burst, our faces grinning with pleasure.) What's interesting is, as I discovered when looking at the pictures Ruo-xin and his brother were showing me after dinner, his father is now sixty-five. Preliberation photographs reveal that he lived in a completely different world during that time. The house they lived in was a mansion compared to the shack they live in now. He wore neatly pressed Western clothing. His father was a landlord.

"His life then . . . ," I said to Ruo-xin.

"Yes, it was very good. But now, he is poor."

"But rich in spirit," I said.

"Yes, rich in spirit."

Photographs turned from the preliberation plushness (for his family, anyway) to postliberation hard times. Building a new country, a new society by first tearing everything down then slowly building it up on an egalitarian set of ideals. Suddenly the clothing in the pictures all turned drab and the same color. The houses were now shacks. Ruo-xin's father's father was dead—he smoked opium until it killed him. They all looked thin and underfed.

Children. As many as the wife could handle. Her first child died as an infant before the 1949 revolution. The Cultural Revolution. All the people in the pictures dressed identically. "This one is gone, too," Mrs. Li said to me, pointing to a round-faced boy in a faded photograph.

Later, Ruo-xin explained to me: "My oldest brother, Ruo-fu, joined his peers and went down to the countryside to carry out Mao's Cultural Revolution. We hadn't heard from him for months when one

day, in 1968, the police arrived at our door with a package that con-
tained his belongings. They said he had committed suicide. I'm
really not sure.

"It was a very chaotic time," he continued. "And because my
family's history was—never mind. Let's not think about it, OK?"

I looked at little Ruo-xin, who was a young adolescent during the
Cultural Revolution, and wondered, how did this time affect him?
Fortunately he escaped the guilt Liu Mei-chun still carries.

"The Chinese are not afraid to eat bitterness," they told me.

Our hands warm and cozy, tucked away in the pocket of his PLA
jacket, we made our way home. "Sing me a song," I said as we
walked through the cold. He sang a song from Mongolia that I love.
Squeezed my hand.

"You seem so happy tonight," he said.

"I am."

I'm glad. If you're happy, I'm happy, too."

On the bus, he looked pensive.

"What are you thinking?" I asked.

"Thinking about what will happen after graduation, my job, the
future."

The future.

Sweet Ruo-xin. Thank you for your friendship.

December 17, 1982

Christ, how much one can learn in one night, or in the past two
days. It's amazing.

We gave a big Christmas party for our Chinese friends last night
and it was a complete flop!

We decorated a huge classroom with lights and streamers and all
that (*I* made the Santa Claus that we hung on the wall—can you
imagine!), and set up a cassette deck with speakers. We had food and
beer, we sang Christmas songs for them. But somehow 80 percent of
them felt really uncomfortable. We even played their kind of music,
danced waltzes, and that kind of thing, but very few of them danced.

What went wrong? I couldn't figure it out. After the party, we all
sat around in the classroom after the Chinese had left and talked for a
while. Two of my Chinese friends had a particularly good time—we
danced and ate and drank. But for most of the others, they seemed

terribly uncomfortable. Why? Even chatting afterwards we couldn't figure it out. All we knew was that the huge culture gap bore its ugly head that night and we all felt disappointed and saddened by its unexpected appearance.

The next day I went to watch a minimarathon that the school was having. Dianne ran in it, as did Carol, Aaron, Harry, and Jeff. Gorgeous day. I tried my best to forget about the fiasco of the night before.

"Hey! Why aren't you running today?" a familiar voice called out behind me. I recognized it as Ruo-xin's.

"What? You're speaking too fast; I don't understand."

He repeated the question.

"Oh! Well, I don't like to race. . . . I don't think you had a good time last night, did you?"

"But I did."

"You guys were uncomfortable, I could see it plain as day."

"Well, oh shit. I don't know. Now it isn't your fault, really. You all gave a great party—but we just aren't used to your kind of parties."

"I understand. . . I think. I don't know, it seems to me that playing, partying, etc., is universal."

"Sure it is. But remember, we had ten years when we couldn't dance or have parties [Cultural Revolution]. That time ended in 1978. It's only 1982. We're still, oh, I don't know."

"I see," I said.

"You know what the problem was? None of us [the Chinese students] knew each other. The students were all from different departments."

"But why does that make a difference?"

"Bai Yu-sha, we aren't like you Americans. We can't just walk up to another Chinese student out of the blue and ask 'who are you?'! I wish we could. But it's too embarrassing."

"Too embarrassing," I thought to myself. "Christ, send me home!" I heard my insides screaming.

He walked me back to the dorm. We chatted about the race, about American music and even laughed a bit recalling the silly awkwardness of the evening before. After that conversation I understood why the party hadn't succeeded.

Actually, the two girls who I'm closest to, Xiao Ming and Yin Zi, had a wonderful time. They're twenty-five years old, started college late because they were sent down to the countryside to work during the last few years of the Cultural Revolution, then worked for a year after that.

Anyway, these women are much older than the others. They know how to relax and enjoy themselves with us. I really have to spend more time with them than I do.

But most of the girls are still at the giggle stage, and the guys are too shy to say boo to any of their female Chinese classmates. Ruo-xin is unusual, particularly in view of the depth and relaxed nature of his friendship with a foreigner—me—who also happens to be female, but he is still very young. It's clear this country had a thick wall around it for ten long years. Only very, very slowly will its effects subside.

In the meantime, my insides remind me, "Don't be frustrated, angry, depressed, confused. Take some of the medicine you're prescribing—relax and try to understand."

With all the strange customs here that I've accepted, I had *thought* my mind was really quite open and flexible. But this party showed me that I have to pry my viewpoint open a few more notches. The trick is to do that without breaking my skull.

The U.S. ambassador invited the American students to his "house" on December 24 to sing carols and all that. I'm looking forward to talking to him. It should be an interesting evening.

In the meantime, I'm going to start building my economics vocabulary. A few words every day will do the job. In a few months I'll be able to listen to a class—one that they *allow* foreigners into, of course.

Lin Yi is terrific. Young. And as she opens up to me, I see a flaming flower, filled with a deep, sweet nectar, endless in its source. She really makes me feel at home here.

After the dance tonight, talking with Fan Long, his calligraphy pens in his hand. He, too, didn't have such a good time and left early. It's a different world here. Amazing.

The guy who taught me the tango tonight was a neat fellow. A good dancer and fairly at ease.

What is Lin Yi dreaming now as she sleeps?

What will I dream? My mind is overflowing with so many things. Letters not written, Chinese characters forgotten, people I want to see, things about myself I have to keep an eye on, the highs and the lows of living here in China.

Why can't I write clearer? Must sleep. Let the dreams wash away all the uneasy feelings. I wish they could do so.

January 1, 1983   *Saturday morning, 9:30 am*

New Year's Day in China.

Well, it's...different.

Last night turned out to be quite nice, dancing at the Jian Guo Hotel, with my American friends. The band was lousy but we danced our fool heads off. Still, nothing compares to the New Year's party that will start in a couple of hours back home in the U.S. It won't be the same this year, of course, as Joey said this morning over the phone. My friends and I won't be there. I wonder what it will be like?

I went downstairs this morning after I washed my hair. Started to dial the operator to call home since I knew they'd all be together tonight getting ready to have lobster. Talking to the operator, about to give her the phone number when all of a sudden an American operator got on the line and asked, "Are you Bessie?"

"Yes!"

"Go ahead, please."

It was Mom and Dad calling just as I was about to call them. We aren't a family for nothing! Twelve thousand miles away, our minds still work in synchronization. It's amazing. Anyway, the first connection was completely worthless so they called back and that was better. They were all there. I could hear the fire crackling, smell the lobster and clams. The warm light of the kitchen. I'm far away today.

Off to Ruo-xin's house to celebrate New Year's with his family. Mom said to tell his parents thank you for being with me on New Year's Day. All the way across the ocean she reaches out to them—to people she doesn't even know but who she knows are important to me. To these people she sent her love. What an amazing woman.

Home. Although I wasn't there in body, I was in spirit. Perhaps too much in spirit. Ruo-xin came to pick me up at ten o'clock that morning to go to his house. We walked out of the dorm into the fresh morning and I burst into tears. I told him I just couldn't come over today, that I missed my family too much. Naturally, in his quiet, gentle way he convinced me to go. No kisses and all that kind of coercion one would find in such a scene in America. This is China. Holding hands is the maximum even after two and a half months.

"If I promise to take you to the Fine Arts Museum this afternoon, will you come?" he asked grinning, knowing that of course I would say yes. It turned out to be a wonderful day. We had an absolute feast for lunch: dumpling stuffed with meat and sage, a mushroom, peanut and garlic tops dish, along with four other dishes—one a cold sweet and sour cabbage dish, the other three vegetables that we don't have back home. One was sort of like a tomato dish but sweeter.

His parents are a riot. I told them Mom's message. The grin on his mother's face was priceless. "They must come visit us!" she said.

"We'll see," I told her. Ruo-xin knows how much I want them all to come and he knows how slim the chance is.

He must have felt my heart vibes at that point because he grabbed my hand and said "Come on! The museum is waiting for us!"

So off we went—saw a somewhat tacky exhibit of ancient stories put into pictures and paintings of modern-day play scenery. The art is very one-dimensional, the medium is used with an amazing lack of creative sense. Everything painted still must support socialist construction. Nothing weird or different is displayed. It's all pictures of model citizens, heroes, stories of good deeds, sufferings, and all that. Ugh. I, however, enjoyed myself in company. He's a good storyteller, and keeps his patience even when I ask him to rephrase every four sentences. The children at the museum were the best part. So cute and playful I wanted to squeeze every one of them. But I restrained myself and squeezed only two of them. Then I looked at Ruo-xin and thought "Hmmm...a Chinese baby might be nice...!" At which point I took the needle out of my arm and we left the museum.

It was a warm day, a nice time to wander around the back streets, through the narrow alleys of the free markets.

Dinner! Another feast, but this one included the food served only on special occasions, chicken. It was sort of stringy, but they absolutely love it. There was fish done in the wok and all sorts of vegetable dishes, plus a clear soup. Ruo-xin's father and I drank the rest of them under the table. After dinner we watched the news on TV, which includes a few more negative stories than the newspaper, but not many. Domestic news is happy news. News from abroad is depicted as chaotic and stories are about recession, war, and so on.

Can't have New Year's without dancing! But the Chinese are just beginning to dance again so most don't know how. It's a strange feeling to live in a country where for so long no one was allowed to dance, and where it is now allowed but strictly controlled through peer pressure and unit supervision at the workplace and in the schools. Rock-'n'-roll dancing is forbidden but still some people do it. Ruo-xin knows how to waltz a bit so we waltzed to the music on the radio and his parents and brother watched and gave instructions. It was a riot.

January 8, 1983

Had an interesting chat with Nancy this morning, the first talk we've had about her upcoming marriage to a Chinese worker. Yes, there are so many choices, so many lives we could lead. She had chosen an interesting one. Damn it, I don't have the patience to write today; so much to say and no will to write it.

Gorgeous day today. I have the first really lousy cold I've had all winter. I shouldn't have gone out walking but I couldn't resist.

I've never had a relationship like this relationship with Ruo-xin. Well, obviously. Jesus, Spero. You've never had a relationship with a Chinese before.

Mr. Li recently explained the family's past to me. His father was a landlord in the northeast part of China. Smoked themselves into oblivion. Mr. Li became an editor of a nationalist newspaper before 1949. So once the antirightist movement of 1957 came, he was severely criticized. In 1966, he was labeled a bad element and a rightist and sent to the destitute province of Shanxi for reeducation and hard labor. There he was imprisoned and allowed to return to Beijing once a year until 1979. After thirteen years of his life had been stolen, the political turmoil ended and he was allowed to move back to Beijing to live with his family.

His spirit is not broken. He is only relieved that he can live out the rest of his days with his wife and children by his side. Mr. Li, you are amazing.

January 9, 1983

I just figured it out, what's been bugging me lately, today talking to Sun Hua and her friend. We went to have Chinese dumplings at Xin Jie Kou. They told me that capitalism was about to die as it is in its highest imperialistic stage right now.

"It's on the downswing now," they told me. "Soon it will be gone." They laughed and then said, as they saw my perplexed look, "We shouldn't discuss this here."

Suddenly I realize why that really gets to me. Here I am, I've come to their country really for one primary purpose and one purpose only: to understand how their system works, how Chinese socialism works economically and politically and socially, how the people feel about it, and how it affects their lives. I've come here only to understand; the Chinese language is but a vehicle to help facilitate my understanding.

Why do I want to understand? Because here is a quarter of the population of the world, a country on the rise, becoming more important and more capable every year. This is a country that the Third World—a growing, developing, and now rightly demanding, set of countries—looks to as a leader. In light of the growing economic and political interdependence between the world's countries, I feel it is important to understand, to *accurately* understand the other countries on which we (the U.S.) depend and who depend upon us.

In addition, we cannot satisfactorily help China—or any country with its development, nor can any two countries interact successfully unless both have a sensitivity and insight into the other's societal, political, and economic make-up.

So, where do I start? I have come to China to live for two years to get the process of understanding started. I came here without a decision on which system I thought was better. Any system will have its good points and bad points. But which one is better is very hard to say. When forced to make a judgment about a country, I tend to place importance on things such as (1) degree of personal freedom of thought and action, (2) whether or not people are starving in their homes and in the streets, and (3) the flexibility and open-endedness of the educational system.

Variety is the spice of life, the spark of invention, and the source of progress in development. Not variety and creativity in clothing or such nonsense, but free-moving, creative, unbound thought and education.

Regardless of the above, I came to China to find out the real story, how this place really works (as much as a foreigner can understand), to get the ball of understanding rolling.

Open.

Ready to listen.

To empathize, to help think out nationwide and worldwide problems.

To share ideas.

To listen.

To let them know, we are not just a big ugly super power. We are ready to work together with them to help develop, enliven, to help save the planet earth and its civilization.

And what comes back in my face?

The top 3 percent of the population, supposedly the best and the brightest, giggling and smiling, their minds locked shut, tight as a treasure chest, telling me my country's system is about to die. They have no understanding of the U.S. society politically or economically and yet they, unlike me, have already made up their minds as to which system is better and which system will not survive.

Jeff's point, however, is well taken. They were never given a chance to think any differently. Their education from day one has pounded their thoughts into their brains with no one around them to offer a convincing or at least interesting alternative viewpoint.

January 13, 1983

Brian found his way into my thoughts tonight. I finished studying for my exam and then put on his tape of songs. Sweet times. I pictured me sitting in the red candlelit bars listening to him sing, watching his spirit soar, watching him sweat and sip on gin and tonics. Sweet love. Take me all the way back, my thoughts. Back even further to wintertime, high school, Bill O'Leary, a boy with red hair, we had red noses, too. Walking in the falling snow. Highland Park High.

And now, a leap through time and I'm walking through the courtyard at school in China. Dusk, smokestacks pumping it out, music and news over the loudspeakers. Lines of students flooding out of the cafeteria carrying bowls of rice and cabbage and tofu. It smells good. They're all chatting away, lively, seeming carefree to my eyes. There's a country on the rise. What is it like to build a country, to be there from its conception?

The snow falls in Highland Park. Bill O'Leary is going off to the library or maybe he's somewhere else. I don't know anymore.

In Boston, Brian is grabbing a quick lunch and then off to one of his million appointments. Did he stop just now? Surprised to find himself thinking about me? Or am I just projecting?

Ruo-xin is sleeping now, just a few minutes down the road. Another new heart, to wander through, to touch, to explore. What is a Chinese heart? This one, filled with spirit and yet an awkward, timid tenderness. A squeeze of my hand and I look up at him. "Thank you for letting me into your life," I say. "Letting my eyes speak for my lips." Correcting my grammar in the moonlight, a combination of learning and loving. Aren't they one in the same today?

I can read the newspaper now, at least some articles, without searching in the dictionary for hours. A whole new world has opened up, or at least there's a door pushed open just enough for me to slip through and see, even if it is with my Western eyes, what's on the other side.

January 14, 1983   *Evening*

If only I could write it all down.

Dianne leaned out of the window.

"Who are you calling?" she said, teasing him.

I grabbed my coat and flew down the stairs. Into the night. So glad to see Ruo-xin. Help! Send me home.

"Come see a movie with me tomorrow.... hmmm?"

"I'd love to," I said.

So he wants to go south for vacation. Fine. Anywhere.

"Are you happy?"

Yes, sweet boy. I am happy.

Family smiling at me on my desk. Beautiful letter from Daddy today.

We walked out behind the dorm, wandering around the construction site. After all the patience, the days of slowly, slowly becoming acquainted. Now he's falling in love. I'm scared. I feel it, a little gnawing sensation inside of me. Real, sweet, sincere feelings, and scary when they're like this: she, an American, two years and then home; he, a Chinese. What are we getting ourselves into?

"Are you comfortable?" he asks me.

Yes, I am comfortable. Astounded at the differences between the Chinese character and the American character. There's one similarity. I feel his passion in his grip.

Must sleep. Must get rid of this cold. Must study. Must enjoy; don't worry. Must not cry. Must read the newspaper every day.

January 18, 1983

It's just a little incident that really got to me. Some goddamn pompous American, Jeff, who happens to speak very good Chinese— who basically associates only with those whose Chinese is excellent. Well, fuck you, boy.

Comes in, wakes up Dianne (a Chinese-American) to ask her if she wants some espresso that he just received from the States. Then offers some to Lin Yi. And then leaves.

I've seen it happen before. This reverse discrimination. Be polite, sweet, and caring to the Chinese and fuck your American comrades. I could scream.

Well, it's just a little thing. The best I can do is make sure I don't do it to my American classmates here. Jeff can go blow as far as I'm concerned.

Ruo-xin's brother works in Xi Dan at a big semi-department store. At dinner on Saturday night he mentioned that the responsibility system was starting at the store. He said he was excited about it, even his father said it was a good thing. I think it'll help all around with attitude and profits. The incentive system at work.

Today the whole school here, every department, is taking the English final exam. It's really wild to think of a whole world of people learning English. I think about why I want to learn Chinese and then why they are learning English, and it's not the same. Ruo-xin says he wants to be able to read U.S. scientific material. Lin Yi wants to read American and British literature. Sun Hua wants to be able to study our production methods and then bring them home to use them. English is in every school here from primary school on up. It's on the TV every night, on the radio, and in the newspapers. My reasons for learning Chinese are not to gather Chinese special talents or methods and then bring them home to use. My motivation is more in the name of easing lines of communication and building mutual understanding (particularly mutual understanding of economic and social problems) in order to enhance cooperation. Because cooperation is the only way to turn off this road that leads to destruction.

I think a bit of a turn to the left in the U.S. would be in order, but

I'm not too sure. If left means sacrificing individuality and personal freedom of thought and action, then there's some rethinking to do.

Is there a happy medium?

I think there must be. The responsibility system that China is implementing is just one example of how they have realized the far left is no good. Of course the far left is no good, as we're reminded in the papers every day. It's a bit of a slide toward the middle—a middle left, if you prefer. Wouldn't it be wonderful if China found that happy medium?

Took a break to get yogurt. Rode our bicycles through the crisp Beijing January air; seems more like late fall in Chicago to me. Pulled up to the store to find a sign that said "1:30—3:00 studying." When we went in at three o'clock, I asked a clerk what they were studying. "The population education program," she replied smiling.

Man, they're experts on spreading material here. You want action? They'll give it you. It's amazing.

January 20, 1983

Nathan's birthday tomorrow.

I sat struggling with my essay at ten o'clock tonight. I got so little done today. Then I heard his voice calling from outside my window.

"Bai Yu-sha!"

"Ruo-xin! Here I come!"

Pulled on my coat and scarf and whipped down the stairs out into the cool night. Smiling, he was wearing his PLA coat. Strolled to our usual place, through the construction site, our own "Love Among the Ruins." He was so happy tonight. He usually is, but he was especially happy tonight.

I felt it inside, too. Sweet, calm, a pleasure.

The moon was setting. I couldn't take my eyes off of it. So bright and orange. And then suddenly, as we stood there, looking at the moon, we saw a shooting star. Bright, clear, swift as it disappeared into the night's black blanket. I didn't know what to wish.

I wanted to wish that we will have a smooth trip.

I wanted to wish that next year will be wonderful.

I wanted to wish. . .

But you only have one. Now that I think of it, I wish for one thing and one thing only. Peace, understanding, cooperation, trust. Peace.

How will we ever work all this out, this crazy world. Is anyone who counts really trying? Or are they just passing through life, making decisions by looking no farther than their shortsighted visions?

Sweet man-child. I'm falling in love with you.

Sleep well.

Well, sleep means dreams, means you and the rest. Sleep well, Daddy. No, you're awake. Well, have a swell day, then. I miss you.

January 26, 1983   *Wednesday morning*

Misty.

The colors are shades of grey and white.

I woke up this morning in a nightmare. Actually, Dianne woke me up; she must have heard me crying out. In the dream, Daddy, Peter, and I were in the basement doing something. The space felt big, like it used to when I was young. We all were listening to Joey, who was upstairs, screaming his lungs out frantically. I guess there was a phone call for Peter. "Why can't we answer him?" I asked Daddy.

"No," Daddy said. "I'm trying to teach him not to scream but to come downstairs and tell us in a nice voice."

"But listen, he's being tortured. You've got to respond to him, please!"

And the next thing I knew, Dianne was waking me up.

"It's just a dream," she said. Whispering in my ear, "It's just a dream."

She handed me a tissue and I cried for a while and then slept.

Later that day

Well, there must be a million and one things I'm worrying about, I don't know.

Vacation. Grad school. Have I picked the field I'm best suited for? What am I best suited for?

Becoming closer and closer to Ruo-xin every day. In the back of my mind searching for a possibility for a way to give us forever. But there seems to be no hope.

A walk in the afternoon today. "If only I had my camera now," he said. Standing by the grapevines, telling each other jokes. Talking about my two American girlfriends who are marrying Chinese men. What makes up a good marriage? No, cultures don't have to be the same, but our love for each other must be strong.

We're going to see an American movie tomorrow.

"In color," he says with a smile!

In color, ah yes, it's the little things.

I hope Xiao Ming does write a play some day. Still, what can she write that would really satisfy her when literature and playwriting are still chained to the post of supporting the revolution and socialist modernization.

Professor Fan—I'm glad to have met him. This should be an interesting one. Why his fascination with Western drama? Because Chinese dramatic development was nothing like it. They have no "tragedy" as we define it, for example.

I suppose I should write less and think less about Ruo-xin and more about grad school and what I want to do. My mind is muddy and thoughts on all of this won't clear. Maybe tomorrow.

January 27, 1983

Finally, today, the first snow has begun to fall. I woke up this morning and discovered the little white flakes silently passing by my window, landing gently on the people and earth below.

My exams being done, I sat leisurely by the window and drank hot, sweetened milk. I thumbed through a *Newsweek* and thought about the snow back home. Crazy girl has to go all the way over to the other side of the world just to see if the snow there can dare to match the beauty of a snowfall back on Oakland Drive. Of course, nothing could be as beautiful as the view of a snowy day from my little room at home, wooden floor, cozy, soft bed. Spacious front lawn, big trees. Brothers to throw snowballs with. Daddy to have cookouts in the snow early on Saturday morning with. Mom to sit in the kitchen with, listen to the radio and talk about our lives, our world, our struggles, our loves. While the snow gently falls outside.

I went out for a walk, leaving my two roommates sleeping happily in their beds. Thought about the last day of classes yesterday and how happy we all were. Professor An told us we did well on our exams, to have a good trip and to come back ready to study hard. After class she and I walked around the field outside the classroom for a while. She told me that on the three exams I did the best in our class, and that she planned to give my final essay to the other professors for them to look at if I didn't mind.

"Your Chinese has progressed so far this semester. At this rate, after a year more of studying you'll speak just like we do. But only if you study hard, consistently, until you leave. You can't afford to get lazy now. This vacation will help your speaking ability in a way the classroom could never do. But when you come back, be ready to work hard." She smiled. "We are all very proud of you."

I thought about the dinner I had with Ruo-xin's family last week. We worked on the itinerary for the trip. Ruo-xin's older brother sat back and smiled.

"You know, during the Cultural Revolution, the trains were free," he said. "Students just got on the trains and rode until they felt like getting off. No matter where they were, they just got off, looked around for a day or two and then got back on the train. You two can do that, too. There's so much to see."

The snow started coming down faster. People on the streets were walking slowly, enjoying the change in the weather, relieved that the snow had finally come.

The Secretary of State is coming to Beijing on Sunday. George Schultz. I'd love to listen in on the talks—wouldn't that be neat? Better yet, I should have Mr. Schultz's job.

"You don't really want his job, do you?" Xiao Ming asked me one day last week.

"Sometimes I do. Really. And then sometimes I just want to be "a worker" have a little house and a child and that's all."

I'm sleepy now.

Sleep calmly, sweet girl. Sleep well.

February 4, 1983

Nanking proved to be more of an adventure than we had bargained for. A night I will never forget.

We paid our 2 yuan each and registered at a small hotel for locals on Liberation Avenue. After dropping our backpacks in our rooms, we set out for a quick evening stroll.

As in most towns in China, the people had turned in early, leaving very little night life for us to observe. Instead we held hands and shared treasured kisses in the shadows. Far away from the confining supervision of the University, the flow of emotion and passion surged out of us and mingled between our kisses, turning our breath into steam as it hit the cool night air. My sweetheart.

Agreeing to meet at the front door at eight o'clock the next morning, we said good night. Sweet smiles. I do love you, Ruo-xin.

The six Chinese women with whom I was to board that night all looked up and stared as I entered the room. They were wide-eyed and amazed to see that they would be sharing the night with a foreigner. I smiled and they giggled, commenting to one another on the new roommate.

"She dresses just like a Chinese," one commented as the friendly evaluation continued.

"How fun!"

"Fun, huh. Well, ladies, I'd love to chat, but I'm exhausted," I thought to myself as I glanced at my watch. Twenty past eleven. Time to sleep. I had just pulled off my boots and was preparing to demonstrate how a Westerner takes off her pants and two layers of long underwear for the anxious audience when there was a knock at the door.

"OK! Is the foreigner in there? Come out immediately," yelled a loud angry voice.

My heart stopped. "This is it," I thought. "They've discovered that Ruo-xin and I are traveling together, he's going to be kicked out of school. Me, I'll be kicked out of China and—"

"Come out immediately!" the voice boomed.

I found myself in a dark back room of the hotel, sitting on a stool with one tall Chinese in a police uniform facing me and another at the door. By the looks on their faces, I clearly had done something that had made them very upset.

"Who are you?" the interrogator asked.

"Cool, stay cool, Bess," I said to myself. "They don't have to know you're with Ruo-xin. Whatever you do, don't mention Ruo-xin. Play it cool."

"My Chinese name is Bai Yu-sha," I answered, trying to look as innocent and naive as possible.

"Give me your passport."

"Shit. No way!" I thought to myself. I took my passport from my purse and gave it to him. He studied it carefully for a few minutes. I waited.

"Can I leave now?"

"No. You're American, I see."

"Yes."

What are you doing in Nanking?" he asked, almost politely.

"Traveling. I'm a foreign student. I'm on vacation."

"I see," he said with a fake half-smile.

"Why do you speak Chinese so well?" his voice turned angry and anxious again.

"I...uh...studied for a long time," I said, lying.

"You're not a student," he said.

"Yes I am," I said, trying to remain as polite and respectful as possible. "Here's my student identification card."

He snatched it out of my hands.

"See? Now, can I have my passport back?"

"No!"

"Son of a bitch," I murmured under my breath. "You can't do this to me." I felt the anger setting in.

"Who are you here with?"

"No one. I'm traveling alone."

"Alone! A woman traveling alone?!"

"Yes," I said, trying to hold back my instinct to tell this male chauvinist pig where to go.

The interrogator glanced at the guard at the door and then back at me.

"What about that Han you came in with? Who's he!" he barked.

"I don't know who you're talking about. I came alone. If you don't mind, I'm very tired and would like to go to sleep."

"Not here you're not. You must leave the city tonight. Don't you know foreigners are not allowed to stay in Chinese hotels? You're supposed to stay in the hotels for foreigners. It's for your own safety. Your things might get stolen here."

He was speaking a mile a minute and I was having trouble following. "I'm sorry, I don't understand."

His face began to turn red. "You don't understand? I don't believe you! You speak Chinese with a perfect accent and yet you don't understand?"

"I'm sorry. I—"

"Listen. You are to get out of this town tonight."

"At eleven-thirty at night? A *woman alone*? I'll leave in the morning."

"You must leave tonight."

"I don't care what you say, you can't throw a person out on the street at eleven-thirty at night."

At that point I stood up, grabbed my passport from his hands, and walked toward the door. "I'll go find another hotel. And I'll tell you, mister, I've never been treated so rudely in any city of China."

"Excuse me," I said to the guard at the door. "I'm leaving."

"No you're not," he said and pushed me back onto the stool. "What are you doing in this city? You're a spy, aren't you!"

"My God. No, I'm not a spy. Look, I'll get out. I'll go to another hotel. I promise I'll leave the city tomorrow."

Later, out on the street, I dropped my pack on the ground and Ruo-xin took me in his arms. My anger turned into tears. I felt confused and saddened. Why? Why all this mistrust?

So, I got in trouble in Nanking. I should have known not to try to live in a Chinese "locals only" hotel. It's done and over with. We left, found me another place to stay, and actually it was quite nice—for only 10 yaun. I was angry, sad, shaken up. Couldn't say much. Poor boy, he tried so hard to cheer me up. I wish he could have stayed, but if we were caught staying together in the same room, all hell would have broken loose.

I slept unusually well after a good, relieving sob session. I just don't understand sometimes.

What I mean is that the rights of the people in China are written somewhere, perhaps, but they are not evenly distributed and they are only there if the higher-ups wish to make them available.

The next morning was a trip out to the Sun Yat-sen Memorial. Built by the Kuomintang, it's the most tasteful, well-built memorial I've seen in China, besides Mao's, and I didn't even go inside that one. The funny thing was, when we were walking around the tomb itself there happened to be a whole mob of peasants and workers from the countryside. There were more of them looking at me and Ruo-xin than at the tomb.

Nanking was quite pretty. The streets were filled with open shops of all sorts, food and knick knacks, but they weren't so amazing to himself—he's used to it—so we only spent a few hours this afternoon wandering around the markets.

The train ride to Suzhou was three hours long—and we stood the whole way. I decided not to bring up his and his family's life during the Cultural Revolution this time because we talked a long time about it on the train ride to Nanking and he obviously felt very sad, unsure, a little depressed afterwards. Talked a lot about the States and where I'd like to live, how unsure I was about which way I wanted to lead my life. Kids on a ranch or a family and career, or what. The ranch sounded peaceful and good for the soul as far as he was concerned.

The late morning was spent walking through the forest, listening to the wind in the trees, and kisses and a bit more. Discovery for him. Pleasure for me to watch him grow and love. He is such a special boy. Not the man I'll marry, our lives will end up worlds apart.

But these few years, our lives meld well. I hope the friendship will last forever. Three hours on a noisy, crowded train and we still can keep each other entertained. There's a good test for you. We'll see.

He's letting me into the heart and soul of a Chinese and I love him for it. And I love him for who he is, his attitude, and the amazingly open mind he carries on his shoulders. I still remember that first time when we went to buy the red coat. . . .

Now we're in Suzhou.

February 7, 1983   *Suzhou, evening*

It does look like a Far Eastern version of Venice. Canals weave in and around the town whose history goes back two thousand years.

Rose at about half past six to wash. Ruo-xin met me in front of my hotel. We spent the day visiting the gardens which Suzhou is famous for. And they were beautiful. We wandered in among the rock gardens, along the lakes, and under the trees. Breakfast, oh yes, oh yes, was rice soup. So tasty and nice and warm; it was a cool, cloudy morning. After finding the map he felt less worried and we spent the day quite content to walk together and see the sights.

Noontime. We walked through the open markets. The peasants were in their native dress. Colorful earrings, well-padded clothing, tunic-type outfits with towels on their heads, sun- and wind-worn faces with bright smiles shining through. The fish they were selling was fresh and attractive. We nibbled on this and that, ate some sweet, strange-tasting pastry, and then headed back to the hotel to get my gloves, which I insisted I didn't need but he said I looked cold and should wear them.

The next hour or so was spent here. Too beautiful to describe. An afternoon love. His first. So joyous. Precious, sharing, loving. Childlike smile.

And then up we rose and out we went to another park, where we bumped into a Chinese tour, a public sort of thing. A man was explaining the history of the place and the crowd seemed to love it, laughing and responding. Finally they have a chance to learn their own history, and they're eating it up.

Dinner. Absolutely scrumptious. Sat on the second floor of a restaurant, run-down, like most of them are in China. Run-down, old tables. Chaotic atmosphere. Cooks running about, people chatting, lively and excited. We watched the the sun go down over the buildings outside the restaurant window.

Went back to get our coats at the hotel and ended up making love. I can't believe how skinny he is; not one ounce of meat on him. But so strong, playful. Every inch of skin on his body like silk to the touch. I've waited so long just to touch him. And when our bodies were bare, we both shook with the excitement. And then, we seemed just to melt into one another. Warm and cozy we were. And content.

It's amazing, the words he doesn't know.

—to make love.

—orgasm.

And then at half past eight, out we went again. Just to stroll along the canals, eat an apple, talk about any old thing. It was a lovely evening. Everyone was out on the streets, selling things, running outdoor restaurants, or just for an evening walk.

Just now we said good night. Until tomorrow morning at quarter till eight, when we'll begin our fourth day. I wish it would last forever. Two kids, free, running around exploring China. Watching her sun set over each city. Riding the trains. Talking to the old men. Making love. And as they grow closer and come to understand one another's culture better and better, so the world is one step closer to understanding and peace.

Wishful thinking? No. The only place to start is where you are. It may be small, but it is one, a start, a beginning. A hope.

Tomorrow I'll write a bit more about the city itself. Got to get a letter off to Mom and Dad.

February 9, 1983

Suzhou was wonderful until we went to catch the boat to Hangzhou. I felt great when I woke up at half past five that morning. We met at the front of the hotel and walked around while the streets of Suzhou wore their early morning colors. People were already out and about, brushing their teeth on their front steps or carrying out the traditional, slow, dancelike movements of Tai Ji Quan in the park. I wanted to blend into their world, stay forever in what seemed such a simple, beautiful existence.

"Two tickets to Hangzhou, please," Ruo-xin said to the ticket seller down by the canal.

The old man peered out from behind the window. "Are you buying for her, too?"

"Yes."

"She can't ride on the boat. She's a foreigner."

"Why can't foreigners take the boat? We're together!" Ruo-xin protested.

"Well . . . the boat's not too safe. Can't risk putting a foreigner on board."

His words hit the ground like bricks. If it's not safe enough for foreigners, how is it safe enough for Chinese? I felt like I was going to be sick. When, when, when, will I be treated as just another person here instead of some honored guest who must be protected and pampered?

Feeling frustrated and disappointed, we made our way back to the hotel. And, as the sun rose to seven o'clock in the sky, comforted in each other's arms, we fell into a deep, satisfying sleep.

The day before, we had climbed a mountain and sat and looked at the blue skies and trees that resembled quaking aspen. Ate pears on the mountain, then maneuvered our way down the rocky paths to the tea house near the bottom.

The countryside out that way is beautiful and the peasants we saw looked strong and healthy, lively.

Hopped on another rickety bus and went to a Buddhist mosque, in use today. Peaceful, set in the mountains. A young monk, a boy, was sitting near a building, cutting green vegetables. An older man tended the garden. A bell, hanging from the temple roof, rang out as the wind came and went, carrying the sound down the mountain.

A gorgeous day was topped off by a mediocre dinner back in town. No matter. The streets were alive. Peasants selling eggs and fruit. People strolling around, enjoying the fresh night air. One American and one Chinese walked hand in hand looking in store windows, staring at the vendors and planning their next day's itinerary.

Now it is nearly twenty-four hours later. The sun is going down over the countryside just outside Hangzhou. The lakes are wearing the pink reflection of the sky. The trees are but black outlines against the rosy background.

Chinese boy, studying his English, sits across from me. His hair is a bit tousled, he looks tired but content. I point out the sunset to him, he looks, smiles, and then goes back to his book. Around the country we wander. With two sets of eyes we see a whole new world of things new to us both. It's true, Chinese and Americans, in terms of attitude, personality, and habits, are worlds apart. But somehow, two, who people say are strangely alike, have found each other. The gaps, even as they are still appearing, grow smaller and smaller because of love and understanding, communication. A friendship that even after I return home will continue. It's a sweet thing that's happened.

The music has come on over the loudspeakers and people are packing up their cups and children, preparing to get off the train.

Time to go.

February 12, 1983

I lean out the window of my hotel room in Shanghai. Music from a popular film floats freely through the air. Firecrackers pop every few minutes. Shanghai. After hearing about it for so long, I'm finally here. It actually looks a lot like New York City probably looked in the 1930s—except with a bunch of Chinese people running around.

Left Hangzhou this morning. As we rode the bus to the train station, we got a good glimpse of the morning chaos, colorful and lively. People brushing their teeth on the street, running here and there with baskets full of fruit and so on. People cooking out on the street, bicycles dodging in and out of the obstacle course provided by the morning events. A few hours on the train, and then before we knew it we had arrived in Shanghai. After a feast at his relatives' house, I'm sleepy and ready to rest. Their house is in the old French quarter where Aunt Tess must have lived in the 1920s. I wonder what this country was like then, preliberation?

One thing this trip had brought to light is the vast differences in the various areas of China. Not only South versus North, but in the South itself there are tremendous differences. Not only in language and eating habits, but personality, attitude, customs, and social interaction on a daily basis also seems to be different in Nanking than in

Hangzhou, than in Shanghai. Take the North and you've got Beijing versus Inner Mongolia—I mean!

More on that tomorrow night.

Lovely day.

February 15, 1983
  Shanghai

The radio says it's Tuesday. As far as I'm concerned, every day is Sunday.

Spring festival in Shanghai.

Ruo-xin just called. Got to go.

February 17, 1983

We would have left this afternoon, but there's no boat to Qing Dao today. So we'll wait one more day. Both of us really have had enough of Shanghai. It's noisy, the air is dirtier than it is in Beijing— and there are too many people. Any time one walks along the streets, main streets in particular, one is surrounded by a mass of bodies. You really can't move without bumping up against one person or another. They are city people. Very well-dressed, fast-moving. The young people are very casual and open on the streets, holding hands, arms around one another, even a kiss or two. A world away from the atmosphere in Beijing. It's time to go.

Visiting the relatives has been quite an experience. Talk about obsession with forcing people to eat! For example, yesterday we went to the people's house who we met on the train from Hangzhou to Shanghai. Beginning with candy and peanuts, tea, cake, then a full-fledged lunch, ten different dishes plus sweet rice cake and ending with New Years cake. We just rolled out of there.

This particular family's life has been hard. During the Cultural Revolution they had relatives studying abroad and the father was labeled as a capitalist. The house was taken, they were shoved into this little place where the brothers had to sleep on the floor. It is a ridiculously small place for nine people to live in. They recalled out loud how none of the children could attend school because all the schools were closed during that time.

Now there are beauty parlors, food-covered tables. Life is better now. But the memory of these ten years is strong and clear. Education is having a revival.

"Everyone went crazy," they tell me.

"It was a terrible time."

February 18, 1983

Spent the morning with Ruo-xin's niece and nephew yesterday. Watched the boats, played in the park, and ate sunflower seeds. Cute kids. Their family situation is apparently not unusual. The father, Ruo-zhi (Ruo-xin's brother), was sent out to Xinjiang to work during the Cultural Revolution. The daughter stayed in Shanghai to go to grade school, mother and son followed Ruo-zhi out west. Once every four years, the government sent Ruo-zhi home to Beijing to visit his parents.

Finally, they've had enough. All together they're moving to Anhui province to be a family again. They don't seem to be bitter at all about their time apart. They do seem somewhat hardened, though. Not the children, but the wife. Ruo-xin says perhaps it's life in Xinjiang that did it to her. I learned that she lost a baby during childbirth there. The umbilical cord was wrapped around its neck and it choked to death. "He was such a beautiful, healthy baby," she said to me, cursing the doctor, the province, the poverty. And the people were apparently very different from where she was raised. No doubt. But I'll have to go out and see for myself.

Seeing Ruo-xin and his little nephew together was a pleasure. They were so happy to be together again, they couldn't keep their hands off of each other. Very affectionate. The whole extended Li family seems that way. Very Jewish in many ways.

Last night was a pleasure. After going to a movie (about the struggle of a few Communists in preliberation time) we went to Ruo-xin's aunt's house. She and her husband live in the old French quarter. We sat and talked for a long time, just about this and that, and then made our way up the narrow steps to the kitchen to make dumplings. Sweet smells began to surround us as we wrapped each one while his uncle cooked the rest of the meal.

Smiles.

A family time.

Flour everywhere.

Hungrier by the minute.

And finally, sat down to eat. Such a delicious meal. Northern dumplings, there's nothing like it. But even better was watching them laugh and joke around together, in the worst of conditions—a cold, dark kitchen—warmed by their love and spirit.

Today off to Qing Dao—by boat! That should be fun. But first we're going out to find some nice silk to send Mom for her birthday.

Too many people here! I'm looking forward to leaving. Missed home terribly yesterday. God only knows why. But I couldn't stay down for too long. He picked me right up and said, "Come on, let's go!" A smile and a hug was all I needed. By the end of the day my homesickness was cured, for the most part. Thank you, my friend, I am forever grateful.

Grateful?... Grateful Dead! God, do I miss them!!

February 19, 1983   *Saturday morning*

We boarded the ship last night. A ship is a ship, of course. But on this travel cruiser from Shanghai to Qing Dao, wake-up call is six o'clock in the morning with a series of triumphant marching tunes. Followed by a speech that reminds everyone not to spit on the floor, only to spit in the designated buckets.

Where was I before I got dizzy and had to stop writing?

Breakfast was noodles and cubes of meat and vegetables—not bad. Afterwards we walked out on deck and watched the ocean at play. I could have stood there for hours. The Chinese Sea. Looked at the map in the game room and talked about my later trips to Xinjiang and Szechwan. Talk about a two-year vacation. Jesus, Spero.

Got dizzy, thought I was going to puke. So I teetered my way back to the cabin, lay down for a while. Ruo-xin put his jacket over me, put some Chinese seasickness medicine on my temples and soon I was asleep.

Woke up feeling fine. And there they were, two cadres, a worker, and Ruo-xin playing cards. Good to see him so at home in the world, with people he knows and with strangers.

"Spitting is an uncivilized custom, comrades!" the loud speaker reminds everyone.

They laugh.

He throws down a card.

"That's it! I'm gone."

Laughter.

I get up to go to the bathroom.

"How are you?"

"Good."

"Good."

I smile. He smiles.

Then I leave him to his card game with the other men.

No, my influence has been positive, not negative. Our mixing of thoughts has not left him unsatisfied with his country and country-people. Even before I came along, he knew what the problems were. This relationship has only opened his mind and my mind to new ways of looking at the world, new habits and customs, and allowed us to enjoy the pleasures of real friendship, which for me is a rare experience. It leaves my soul happy and relaxed. A good state of mind for coping with living in a foreign country and learning a foreign language.

After watching the movie about the Communists' preliberation struggle, I asked how many people in China he felt would like a change in government. I can't ask too many people this question.

His response, of course, comes from a somewhat isolated university student's viewpoint. Still, it sounded accurate to me. "A lot of people really want to have a capitalist system," he explained. "A lot of young people really want it. I'd say perhaps half the population wants a big change."

Then there are those that like the present system of government but want some particular changes, which are beginning to happen, slowly but surely.

"And you? What do you want?"

"I don't really like the capitalist system. It leaves too much room for selfishness and corruption. But I'm not satisfied with China's present system either," he said.

"So you don't want capitalism, you don't want socialism, you want a new 'Chinese-style' government, huh?"

"Perhaps that's my meaning."

He doesn't believe that attainment of true communism is possible. "It's only theory; it will never happen."

Lin Yi doesn't agree.

Change, how to bring it about?

"It's not worth talking about," Ruo-xin says. "What I say, what my neighbors say, doesn't make a difference. It's no use."

"Then what will bring about the big changes?" I ask.

"I don't know. . . . Before the Cultural Revolution a lot of people felt really concerned and involved. Everyone talked about politics all the time. But now, we just each tend to our own affairs. It's the only way to survive."

Christ.

Lin Yi explained to me a few weeks ago, just before I left for vacation, about one of the lasting effects of the Cultural Revolution. During the revolution, you couldn't trust anyone with your inner thoughts. If any of your feelings were not of the correct line, the accepted thought, then you couldn't express them—even to the closest of friends. Why? Because everyone felt that everyone else was a potential tattletale who would report any suspicious words or actions. And then there would be trouble, real trouble. Ruo-xin, Lin Yi, and their peers were very young at the time, but the influence of the time still lives in their insides as well. Deep feelings, from emotions to political sentiments, are not to be shared. Or, if they are shared, they're to be told only to select friends who can be trusted. People are still a little afraid. Some, of course, more than others.

Some are just numb.

Last night, Ruo-xin and I came back to the cabin to sit for a while.

"You're interested in philosophy?" the cadre asked me in broken English.

"Yes, why?"

"I noticed your book on Marx."

Then he launched into a tirade on Marx being all wrong and it was Hegel who was right. His English was poor and I didn't quite understand. Then he told me how lucky I was to live in a democracy.

"I wish we had it here," he said. "It's the best way."

"But the peace movement in the West," he said, ". . .it's all wrong!"

"Why?" I asked.

The gist of his argument was that the peace movement calls for stopping construction of war weapons. If the U.S. stops producing war weapons, then we have nothing to fight the Soviets with. "Look at Poland! The workers have no weapons. They're going to lose."

"The Communists, they are. . .bad." It was the only word he knew, but the expression on his face said "hateful." He continued, "We must fight against them. With weapons. If we have no weapons, we are lost."

"Change. Does change have to come about by way of war?"

"Yes."

At which point I started speaking in Chinese to move the conversation along a bit faster. Suddenly he turned white and said, "Please, only speak in English," and quietly left the room.

Today we met in the corridor. "Please don't tell anyone my words. I am a Party Secretary."

I assured him I would tell no one. I guess he took a big risk. Now here's an authority directly confronting government policy—not on the Soviet issue, but on the issue of democracy. Change *can* happen here.

"Let's not talk about it here in the cafeteria," Ruo-xin says.

Then he pulls out a map of Qing Dao. "Let's see now, where should we go?"

OK. OK. Let it go. I guess I don't understand.

March 1, 1983

  Beijing

The radio preaches about the way to be a good socialist student. The colors outside my window are shades of greys and whites and blacks. Bicycles passing by, ringing their bells. The firecrackers from the New Years celebration have stopped. It's back to work here in Beijing.

I'm glad to be back, as wonderful as the vacation was, as free as our lives were those three weeks. Off to class.

March 3, 1983

Tomorrow is Mom's birthday.

In like a lion out like a lamb. Is the rule right?

Not here. It's raining this morning. Temperature is mild.

Although I went to bed at one o'clock last night, I couldn't sleep past six-thirty because of a person above me sweeping the floor and moving chairs around, etc. Ah, well. No matter.

March 5, 1983

Had our farewell dinner tonight. Farewell, sweet Chinese roommates! You have given us the most precious gift anyone could ever give—the gift of language. Communication.

When we first came, we could barely say a complete sentence. And now? Anything goes. They were so patient, such good teachers.

I sat with Wang Quan Sheng at dinner. Sweet smiling face. I remember when I first met him. His smiling eyes were the first thing I saw. His classmates don't understand. Don't they see? He's just as spirited, as human, as warm as the rest. Ah, well. Human misunderstanding goes on and on.

March 7, 1983

Ruo-xin's birthday.

Yesterday: a day one first wants to remember, then wants to forget. God bless it! Well, the morning was depressing only because Dianne woke up depressed again. No energy, still felt sick. I gave her some water. She sat and drank, didn't say much.

But at noon, I didn't care. I hopped on my bicycle and went to Ruo-xin's house. A beautiful blue-sky day. Walked down Wang Fu Jing and felt fine. Went to Tian Tan Park, a huge, forested park where the emperors used to play. The Echoing Wall and all that. It had been a long week of work and ups and downs—particularly with Dianne finally coming back from Guilin yet so ill, and the strange feelings that came with Mom and Dad's offer to help me come home for a while this summer. I still don't know what I'm going to do about that. But at Tian Tan, we relaxed, enjoyed watching the people flying kites, sat and drank soda, relaxed.

Walking through the park, we came upon a grove of pear trees. It seemed as if someone had put it there just for us. In a country plagued by overpopulation, there is rarely a single piece of ground where two people can find real privacy. But there in front of us was a grove of pear trees without a soul in sight. A dream come true.

We walked into the grove and chose a tree to rest under. Ruo-xin looked around nervously until he finally consented to being pulled onto the ground next to me.

"Don't worry," I reassured him. "There's no one around. Don't you want your birthday present?" I asked, laughing. He smiled, looking embarrassed and yet eager.

"Happy birthday, lover," I said.

"Happy birthday," he said, mimicking my English.

Thank you's with kisses. The world around us faded away as we fell into an excited embrace. So seldom could we so freely allow our bodies to press together, to enjoy the electricity that occurs as hands find their way past the confines of clothes.

I didn't realize we had been followed but I was soon to find out. He came upon us from behind. In plain clothes, the policeman stood towering over us.

"A foreigner?...Are your foreigners?"

We sat up, petrified.

"No, I'm Chinese," Ruo-xin said.

"Come with me."

It took me a while to get the leaves out of my hair. It will take me many years, if ever, to get the knots out of my stomach, the anger out of my heart. Just two minutes alone, damn it! Can't anybody even have that? The people here have no rights. It's amazing.

He took Ruo-xin far down the road to question him in privacy. They talked for what seemed an eternity. What were they saying? Negotiating a settlement?

"Come with me," he barked at me as they came walking back down the road.

"Sit here."

"No, thank you. I'll stand."

"As you like. Now, answer clearly. Did he feel your breasts? Did you have an orgasm with him? Answer clearly!"

"No."

The questioning went on. He wanted every detail. With each response, his face grew redder and redder. I could see his penis hardening and rising under the zipper of his pants.

"You disgusting schmuck," I thought to myself.

I stopped answering the questions. "That's all," I said with a strong bite in my voice. "I'm not answering any more of your questions. Can we go now?"

"The kind of behavior you two have engaged in is uncivilized. It's against the law, you know."

"We didn't break the law. We've done nothing wrong. You're not going to report us, are you? Please...don't do that." I started to plead with him. Reporting us would mean Ruo-xin's expulsion from school.

He gave no answer.

"Perhaps you allow this kind of activity where you come from, but we are a civilized nation of people in China."

Civilized? I thought I was going to be sick. I kept reminding myself: Don't get angry, Basha. It will only make things worse. Hold your burning tongue.

He finally let us go. We made our way back to the entrance of the park and out into the crowded streets. The sun was going down as we squeezed onto the bus. Neither of us uttered a word on the way back to school.

I pity the young people who are stuck here forever.

March 10, 1983

I do as much as I can, and still it's not enough. Work all day, and I still can't read the goddamned newspaper! I'd really feel distressed if these days hadn't been so fine. So fine. I think I miss home a bit today, but it's only because they played Gershwin over the loudspeakers on campus tonight. I adore Gershwin. And I miss the culture of the Western half of the globe.

There's nothing quite like Thursdays—when I have economics class. Actually, it would be better to say that there's nothing like going to class with the Chinese. In an old run-down classroom they sit and learn. Sitting behind a broken wooden desk on top of an ugly cement block sits the professor who bows respectfully to the students as they stand at attention. Sure, some listen to the lecture, and some read work for other classes. Just like American students. This professor happens to be really lively, young, enthusiastic, and conscientious (how the hell do you spell that word?). Yapping away in clear Mandarin. I understand about 50 percent, sometimes 70 percent, of it. Xiao Ming helps out, sitting next to me. At break time, Yin Zi and I went outside with everyone. Springlike weather. They were all out there doing their exercise routines. I love it.

So many hurdles this country has to leap. And my friends, my friends have to live here without the freedom I know—or the freedom I think I have.

My insides are so filled with—with everything.

Gershwin.

The back porch at home.

Grandma's letter.

Walking around campus. The girls from Xinjiang on campus.

Mixed feelings about my discussion about communism with Fang Zhi Hua last night.

Wondering how to see past my own notions, how to open up to their thoughts.

Thoughts of Ruo-xin, loving him and his friendship. Missing him already and I haven't even left.

Early morning exercise.

Afternoon nap.

Rice, so satisfying, noodles.

Studying—I see the results every day, concrete.

Evening strolls.

Coffee.

Mom. Dad.

My boys, Peter, Joey.

Sweet Sal.

China.

Home.

My insides feel like bursting.

Forget it, go to the classroom.

Study.

Enjoy the company of your friends with slanted eyes. Laugh, girl, make it. You can, for just a bit longer. I love it and at the same time...

March 16, 1983

Looking back on that entry, it must have been the music that did it to me.

This week seems to have gone much faster than last week. God, last week dragged on so! I guess I was getting used to the new work load.

Spent the afternoon (after a good nap—what a wonderful custom) in the classroom with Ruo-xin. The wind was up to high speeds today, fierce and cold, penetrating the walls of the math building where we studied. We all sat with coats on, hunched over the wooden desks. I just about froze, and although the Chinese students are fairly used to this kind of physical abuse, they felt the cold, too.

Still, one girl hummed away as she took a break around four o'clock, some read the newspaper, Ruo-xin took my hand secretly underneath the desk and smiled. I finished up another section of the Lu

❖ *My first glimpse of China—the guard at the border between Hong Kong and China.*

❖ *The train is the most popular—and for most Chinese the only—way to travel long distances in China. Here's the Canton to Beijing train, August 1982.*

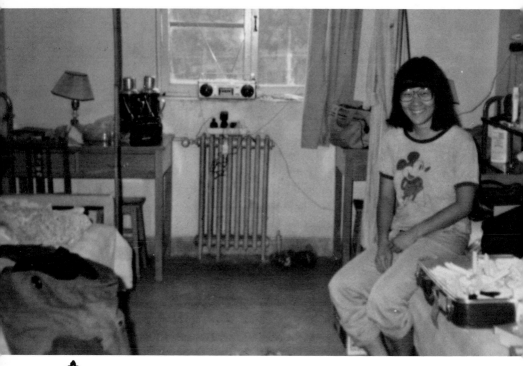

❖ *Dianne in our room at Shi Fan University in Beijing shortly after I arrived in August 1982.*

❖ *My dorm room my second year at Shi Fan University, August 1983.*

✧ Top: *Here is the building at Shi Fan University where Ruo-xin and I met in 1982.*

✧ Above: *Foreign students came from the Orient as well as the West. Here I am with two Japanese friends in my dorm room in 1983.*

✧ Below: *Some friends in front of the cafeteria at Shi Fan University in 1984.*

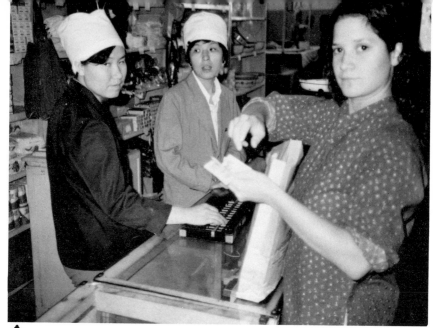

❖ *Shopping in Beijing in early spring 1983.*

❖ Below: *Inside my hut in Mongolia on my trip there in the winter of 1983.*

✦ Above left: *Shanghai harbor is in the background of Ruo-xin and his relatives, whom we visited in February 1983. From right: Ruo-xin, sister-in-law, nephew and niece.*

✦ Above right: *We visited Suzhou, the Venice of China, on our trip to Shanghai in the winter of 1983.*

✦ *Here I am hunting for Chinese scroll paintings at the arts and crafts district in Beijing.*

✥ Above left: *Ruo-ji hitting the books at home.*

✥ Above right: *Mr. Li at the Li house in Beijing.*

✥ Below: *Mrs. Li and Ruo-xin's brother, Ruo-ji, at the Li house.*

✤ *Dinner, with chop sticks and all, at the Li's. Meals there were a nice break from the university cafeteria.*

✤ *Live chickens are just one of the goods for sale at this Beijing market near Shi Fan University.*

❖ *Ruo-xin on one of our many walks through the Summer Palace in Beijing.*

❖ *The Li family gathers at the train station to say goodbye to Ruo-xin and I as we head to the States in July 1986.*

Xun story ("Kong Yi Ji") and learned about thirty new vocabulary words. It was a good afternoon.

The trip this summer sounds more and more tempting every day. I never had the desire to visit the Soviet Union before, not to mention Czechoslovakia or Yugoslavia. But now my curiosity has been piqued. Which means it's time to go look.

Christ, I'm still freezing.

Today I found out that the girl who jumped from the girls' dormitory yesterday morning succeeded in killing herself. Apparently she "lost face" in a love affair. People are crazy wherever you go.

March 22, 1983

I feel better now—after a long, emotionally up-and-down day. I ran tonight and then took a shower. That's better.

I think it must be a million things that are upsetting me. Hormones at their peak as I'm just about to get my period. Breasts, Christ, so painful I could scream sometimes. I hope this Chinese medicine works to melt the steel knife that seems to penetrate my nipples whenever it chooses to do so.

I woke up two mornings ago, too aware of the dream I had had. It's almost too hard to write it down. Daddy had died. No one told me until days later. I can't begin to write down how I felt. Empty, devastated, amazed, I guess.

Ruo-xin. Sometimes I think I'll be bored before I know it. Or he'll be frustrated with my strange ways and then, bam. It will be over. So, I've gone through it before, what's once more? There's a heart inside of me that's just beginning to heal. She needs more time. A hurt right now would be—too much. I'd have to sleep for a long time to get my feet back on the track. And then again, maybe not.

But why the hell am I thinking like this?! Crazy girl, you're happy now. Enjoy it, enjoy him, enjoy the support and strength of the love the two of you have found.

Was it by chance?

A bright morning?

A red coat?

Two loving souls.

Fang Zhi Hua has been a treat. We are so alike in so many ways. It's startling.

Mornings—early to rise.

Evenings—early to bed.

A hard worker, and yet, time to chat. To see a movie by herself is fine. With a friend is good, too.

From Fang Zhi Hua: "Remember, all Chinese people are not alike. There are so many of us, how could we all be of the same temperament, same attitudes, same ideas?"

I never knew two people of such different cultures could be so alike.

Saw Lin Yi tonight. She seemed flighty and snotty. And then I looked closer and noticed she was waiting for a sign from me. For a look. For a smile. I caught her searching in my eyes for a glimpse of love. Sweet Lin Yi, you'll never know how much you've meant to me. But with all of your defenses and all of my insecurities, we'll never be able to bring back those wonderful talks in midafternoon and late at night. Still, we shared a special time, and I won't forget you. Nor will I forget your pride that you had for yourself and for your country. Fang Zhi Hua is also that way as is Ruo-xin, but not quite so much.

Fang Zhi Hua wants to be a translator. I think she'll be one some day. Perhaps. Anyway, she offered to translate my book when I write it. It's not such a crazy notion. I'd really like to write about my first two years here. But there has to be a particular focus to it—a catch to it to attract people to read it.

Wonderful tape from Mom that I listened to this morning. The Dixieland music made my insides turn upside down.

God, I miss home.

April 8, 1983

I could really kick myself for not writing for the past two weeks. And trying to recount it all is next to impossible.

Spring has arrived. The forsythia and the peach blossoms are blooming. Color. Real color! There was a precious afternoon when we walked around the campus flower garden and then stood in front of the foreign students' cafeteria as the sky turned pink and the sun began to slip down behind the buildings of the town. The flowers opened up for us and let their sweet smell fill the spaces around us. Heaven is here on earth, sometimes.

We passed over a rough spot. I'll never know exactly what it was. But it was strange and frustrating and just wanted to split this country. It's over now.

I'm in limbo. The trip to the Soviet Union is all set. Moscow, Leningrad, Rega, and then the Black Sea coast. All I need is to get this job and then I can go. But the chances don't look too good right now, and I may have to revamp my plan. Speaking of revamping, Dianne was rejected across the board by all the graduate schools she applied to. She's taking it fairly well. It does force her to change her plans a bit. A year from now, will I be in the same position? I really want to go to grad school—I haven't gotten enough education to satisfy me. I've really just begun. Just towards the end of undergraduate school I figured out how to study and how to make it stick. And just as I got it all straight, it was May 1982, and I had to leave. I sat in the car and Daddy drove us through the campus and then through Medford, and finally out to the highway. Fade in, fade out, fade in: I'm on the plane from L.A. to the Orient.

Enough daydreaming. I just hope I get accepted to grad school, that's all.

We took off in the middle of the week last week for dinner at a place in Xin Jie Kou. Sat and talked about Deng Xiao Ping and how much power he has these days. Zhao is meeting all these visitors at the airports; Deng is behind the scenes making policy. He has been in the paper recently. Once planting trees for "Beautify Beijing" month, once for his meeting with Tip O'Neill. Ruo-xin seems to think that Deng is still playing quite a role, even though he no longer holds the official post of leader of the Communist Party. But no one really knows. There is one thing we can say for sure and that is Hua Guo Feng is not exactly playing anything near to a crucial part in the present Communist Party. He unfortunately bears the mark of Mao's favorite; that ruins his career right there.

Ruo-xin was telling me how every household had a picture of Mao on the wall.

"Even your house?" They're not exactly the politically concerned types.

"Even my house. Of course, we had to."

The question remains, how did they know when they could take it down? Professor An told us another section of the Cultural Revolution: the time out in the countryside.

"There were no leaders around to order us to work, so we didn't work." The harvests were meager as a result.

"Time to come to distribute grain and the small amounts of money—and there was barely enough to go around.

"We sat in the fields and talked...for years. And then, finally, it was over and I went back to school.

"Some people stayed in the city to take part in the revolution, they smashed the windows of the school buildings. Campuses became battle grounds. I just didn't want to be any part of it."

"I remember not understanding why I couldn't go to the park; Mama and I used to go all the time," Ruo-xin said, "and then one day it was closed."

He was in middle school at the time. Apparently it didn't close.

"We spent a lot of time reciting questions from Mao's red book and marching in the streets. Everyone had a gun to hold on his shoulder as we marched. We all thought it was a game! We didn't study very much at all, really.

"On the weekends we got on the bus and went out to the countryside, supposedly to work in the fields next to the peasants. But no one ever worked. We just played all day."

But it wasn't all rosy for this child in Beijing.

"Dad was gone most of the time, since he was sent out to the countryside to serve hard labor. Mama and I never really had quite enough to eat—but no one did. It was a confusing time. The classroom was a zoo. Mama had to attend self criticisms all the time. I didn't understand what we had done wrong. I remember missing my father and my sister."

Paranoia.

"What about the peasants who felt like everyone should work so that there would be enough food for the following year? Did they ever speak up?"

"They were afraid to. Everyone was watching everyone else. You really couldn't trust anyone. It's better now, though."

I can still see the remnants of the paranoia, though. It's plain and clear.

There's a college in China that's starting a special set-up for their graduates. They won't be assigned a job by the government but, with the help of the school, they'll look for work themselves. New laws are being passed to protect the individual rights of the peasants to have their own tractors, sell their own produce, and run their own businesses. And then I sit in economics class and he talks about the importance of a planned, controlled economy. I've never seen so much diversion between theory and practice as what's going on now—particularly economically.

The spring dust storms came this week. And then last night, the rain came. Sweet, fresh, and wet! What a relief.

April 9, 1983

In the *International Herald Tribune* I read about how Mr. Reagan wants to tighten controls over technology exports to prevent the passing on of high technology to the Soviet Union. I have such mixed reactions when I read something like that.

My gut reaction is "That's a schmuck move, Mr. President. Paranoia feeds on paranoia, which feeds on paranoia. Mistrust works the same way. If we don't trust them, they'll never trust us and vice versa."

But then isn't it true that security for one must mean insecurity for the others?

Does it always—from now until forever—have to be that way?

Another reaction: "The Soviets are opportunistic. In light of that, we can't risk sharing our own technology when it might be used against us."

It's true that history looked at in one light shows the Soviets to be opportunistic. But looked at in another way, they have many reasons to see us as the same, and they therefore must cover their bases, lest they be the next object of *our* opportunism.

It's craziness.

Were we all meant to destroy each other, or what?

Speaking of craziness, I got a letter from Cath today. We're so far away, I don't even know where she's at any more. I look back at Tufts now and realize how lonely it can be if you don't have a close friend or lover. It's not like here where everyone lives with five other classmates. You work, eat, sleep, and play together, where the collective spirit is encouraged and mutual support stands as the model method for everyday relations. It not only is theory, but it also works in practice here inside the university walls.

Outside on the street is another story.

April 10, 1983

Jesus. I'm unfaithful even to the best man I've ever found. I don't know what it is. If there's a hell, I've got my ticket booked.

April 11, 1983

At breakfast this morning, I sat with one of my Japanese businessmen classmates and talked. The discussion began with his comment that a lot of the American students were frequently skipping class, whereas the Japanese still had full classes.

Then moved on to the Hu Na incident.

"You realize, if U.S.–Japanese relations go sour, it has a big influence on Sino–Japanese relations," he said to me.

"Although we may be called an independent nation, we really aren't in so many ways. We still have to follow the American moves in terms of foreign policy. If your relations with China cool down, ours must as well. If the U.S. doesn't attend the Olympics, then Japan can't, either. U.S. Army and Navy people are still in every city. During the Vietnam War, Japan was a launching pad for the U.S. Army."

"I'm sorry."

"I am too—but don't worry, it's not your responsibility."

April 13, 1983   *Wednesday*

Went out for my morning run. The weather has turned warm—a pleasure. Ruo-xin was playing basketball. I ran around the track, watched the flowers bloom. A hundred black heads converged around the podium by the side of the track. Quite a sight.

Back at the room, drinking coffee, eating a pear, home came into my thoughts. It was this time last year that Mrs. Newman died. Leila,too, was killed at this time last year. The flowers were blooming, bees buzzing. One stung Beth as she walked over to the funeral on that April day.

If only I could see Sal for just a minute, just one minute to hold her and tell her I love her, absorb some of her pain. Bob, Nancy, Ricky, do you all know I'm thinking of you? So many times you find your way into my room here across the ocean. Just a little while longer and we can be together again.

A sweet note from Ruo-xin last night while I was studying: "I love you. I want to kiss you right now."

April 17, 1983   *Sunday, late afternoon*

After an eon of uncertainty and then a day touring a model Chinese oil refinery, the answer of "No" came about the job for next fall. The Soviet trip slipped out of the realm of possibility as I opened up and then read Daddy's letter which sent disappointment but also a lot of love. Suddenly I didn't want to leave Beijing even for a month, for a day, for even an hour this summer. I want to stay, study, and walk in the park. And I still might do it.

April 21, 1983

So, there you go. Spent at least two or three weeks screwing around over what to do for the summer break. Jesus. When will I ever grow up? When will I ever stop missing home? When will I ever stop spending so much time thinking about tomorrow? It's not easy to change.

Talked to Joey this afternoon. Sweet boy. So good to hear his voice. Still, sometimes I think phone calls are just useless. Just makes me miss everyone.

This entry is useless. Forget it.

April 22, 1983   *Friday afternoon, 5:00*

The best days in the world are Friday afternoons.

No, I didn't let the nasty headache that started last night ruin this day. I woke up this morning and my head was still throbbing. So I went back to sleep. Half past twelve, woke up to a gorgeous blue-sky day and a sweet spring wind coming in through the open window. And my headache was gone.

Spent an hour or so going over yesterday's economics lecture with Xiao Ming in an empty classroom. Helped the cleaning woman wash off the window sills and we then chatted awhile. Then, off to watch the all-school sports meet, which started this afternoon. Ruo-xin was refereeing for some event that I don't know the name of. I sat on the fence and watched the girls run. Young, healthy bodies. And they're all virgins—it's amazing. Now, Bess, really, must you make comments like that?

When himself was finished, he came over to talk for a while. If it had been Nathan he would have said "Do you want to have dinner in the city tonight and then go to a party at Fletcher?" Ruo-xin's version of same was, "Are you coming to the classroom to study tonight?" I really wanted to giggle. But I only smiled and said, "Sure." It's not quite like a dinner in Boston but it has it's good points too.

Later on, back at the dorm, I realized I had forgotten my bicycle at the field, so I went back to get it. Passing by the fenced-in area, I saw some boys from the biology department practicing Tai Ji Quan. These grown-up fellows, just as masculine as any other guy, immersed in a dance of graceful, flowing movements. I stopped to watch for a while. Just beautiful they were. One spotted me watching them and he smiled.

11:00 that night

Let's not try to write it all down. It doesn't come out accurately when I try to put everything on paper, all in one sitting. I came back from the movie. (I watched but a half an hour of it, twenty minutes of which was spent talking to Cai Jie about bicycles, to Little Hu and a Japanese classmate.) Headed back to the classroom to study, but never got there. Ruo-xin was in the courtyard waiting for me.

You know, the conversation we had tonight was bound to happen to us. With two people whose characters are so similar in so many ways, with two people who have found a real love—they're bound to end up searching for a way to spend their lives together. As I recall, up until now, I had been aiming for a career woman's life. Fulfillment in a job and education comes first, love and husband comes after that. But isn't it amazing how things can change? Honestly—how easily it rolls off the tongue, once it becomes a part of me. For a love, I would even live here in China, wait for him to graduate,...and then? I didn't think he'd be willing to go to the U.S.—but apparently now he is.

What happened? It's hard to say. I'm not sure anyone understands this story, though it's happened time and time again. A girl plans, hopes, schemes about education and career. The man she loves comes along and then, boom, life and plans have changed overnight. Jesus. I still remember the first day Dianne introduced us.

The best laid plans of mice and men. Someone new hits the scene and everything looks different. Is it true that you'll ever sacrifice your graduate education for him? Perhaps so. But then what kind of a job do you expect to find with only an undergraduate degree? That's a good question.

I look at the picture of my family and wonder when I will see them again. Will it be yet another two years?

Some realities: my visa runs out in a year. Then what? How to renew it?

There is a man here—and still a young man. I have found in him a truly caring, faithful love; a natural, mutual understanding. Someone who I am willing to give all I have for his happiness, and a soul who is willing to give all he has for my happiness. Aren't these the things that count? So I told him, "One year from now I'll be going back to the U.S. And I want you to be with me forever."

It's twelve-thirty at night. My life is changing before my eyes. I could choose so many ways to live it. But there is a woman inside of me who wants to live it with Ruo-xin.

He spoke with great concern about my parents and their possible reactions. My family. Sweet family. Will this hurt them beyond description? If I have really found the love of my life, won't they be happy? Of course—and yet, equally as sad that I ever set foot on this continent. How could I do that to them? This is a question I must consider. It is perhaps not worth hurting them so. But if Ruo-xin and I come back to the States, then. . .

What about marrying a man with the same cause? A revolutionary out to remedy the injustices of the world. Ruo-xin is not a revolutionary. Isn't that something you felt was crucial? In one life it is—in another life, perhaps it's a different story. A cause? Isn't the real cause of every person to help her family and children live a happy life? It could be. Now what happened to the cause of peace in the world?

Which life shall I choose?

Or does one really choose? Perhaps it just happens.

How I can go to sleep tonight is a wonder to me. We'll give it a try. Just remember one thing. If you—or he—decide that getting married is not the way to go, remember that your friendship will be forever, and that is a rare and precious thing in itself. If I marry him, this will be a very interesting life, indeed.

April 23, 1983

Early Saturday morning, woke up and couldn't fall back to sleep.

Silly girl. I fell asleep last night thinking about the loans I'm supposed to pay off once I'm out of school for nine months.

My mind is clearer in the morning. Perhaps I'd be happiest just going back to the States to school. Me. A single, independent entity. Enjoying studying, which was my first love for as long as I can remember. Or was it just a replacement? Something to keep me happy until I found the man I love? No, I don't think it's a replacement. But, Bess, remember what Mom said: You don't ever stop learning, even after you stop going to school.

Ruo-xin mentioned the letter we had written in Suzhou to Mom and Dad. "I promised to give you back after another year," he reminded me.

Well, it'll perhaps be two years. And then they'll not only get me, they'll get Ruo-xin, too. We could live with them back in the States. Jesus, what new world I'm dreaming up.

Afternoon. What would it be like for us to go back and live with Mom and Dad in Highland Park? All four of us living together. How would Ruo-xin react to living in that town—once he really got to know it? I just don't know, he perhaps might be more accepting of it than I. I would love to live with Mom and Dad. And I know they'd love Ruo-xin.

April 24, 1983   *Sunday*

Went out to Dong Ling today. The group was a nice mixture of Japanese, five Americans, and our professor. Professor Shu even came along, as well as his son who speaks wonderful English. Sweet Professor Shu—for a man who's taken his share of criticism for not supporting the revolution, he sure has come out of it with enough strength left for an army.

As far as I'm concerned, the best part of the trip was the ride (four hours) out and back. To roll along through village after village, watching the peasants at work is a thrill in itself. There they were, cows and oxen pulling plows, old and young working in the green fields, their heads protected from the sun by wide-brimmed, oriental-style straw hats.

The villages were filthy and the stench has become even worse now that the warm weather is here. They're all out on the streets, playing or selling their wares, chickens and pigs running all around near the outdoor restaurants which are selling sweet fried dough and jasmine tea. Quite a sight. One of the villages nearest Dong Ling seemed a bit better off than the others. Their houses even had glass in the windows.

Now when Professor An tells stories about life in the countryside, I can picture in my mind what the place really looks like.

Dong Ling? Well, I enjoyed walking around with Fang Zhi Hua, making nasty comments about the emperor and all his concubines and watching her blush. What a riot.

The tombs themselves weren't so amazing. What I found interesting was watching the Chinese flood into the area, taking pictures and soaking up the history that has been kept from them for so long.

After we got back, Arthur, Dianne, and I went to the Beijing Hotel for dinner. I sat at dinner and watched Arthur, thought about his career and his research here in China, and wondered if that was what I really wanted. I just don't know. I've got a strong feeling that there may be something a big step higher on the ladder of priorities: family, the man I love. Then again, if your job is lousy, it can be a difficult existence. There must be a balance somewhere.

But when I got back to school, Ruo-xin managed to lift my spirits. They were all in the classroom practicing "collective dancing." Chatted with a few girls and then we went out for a short walk.

"We can *eat the bitterness* (translation: endure the suffering) when it comes along," he told me. He had been pondering over it all day, pondering over us for God knows how long.

Sweetest you, I hope bringing you to the U.S. is the right thing to do. Just because I love you, will you be happy there? Will the competition drive you up a wall? Will you miss your home too much to bear? Will you despise the children that your children go to school with? Will you feel ashamed when you discover that you don't have enough money to send your children to college? Will my love be as precious to you then as it is to you now? That is one thing I can be sure of. However, one can't be sure of too much else.

I am exhausted. Must sleep. Take it slowly, day by day, girl. And enjoy.

April 25, 1983

A rainy Monday. Baroque music and the rain softly coming down outside. A light to study by. A love in my heart. Freeze the moment if you can; keep it in the freezer and take it out to taste it whenever you need to.

Wrote a letter to the boys today telling them about Ruo-xin and me, our plans to be married here in China, and when we would be coming home.

Is all of this real? Or have I lost perspective somewhere?

April 27, 1983   *Daddy's birthday*

Wednesday evening.
A round, white moon.
A misty night.
An evening stroll.
"I've decided," he said, "I want to marry you. Are you willing?"
"I will marry you."
Sweet love. I hope I can make you happy. It's a little hard to believe. Who would have thought on that train from Canton to Beijing, almost a year ago, as we sped along through the countryside? He who was waiting here for me. What will our life together be like? Two vastly different cultures found two people, who fell in love. Suddenly a love takes the place above all else.

For so long I have been obsessed about protecting my independence. Needing someone so much, allowing myself to need in this way, I felt, would be a loss of my self. "Don't let yourself get sucked in," I used to say to myself. "You have so much more life to live." But now I know, needing someone and giving in to that feeling does not mean a loss of independence. Needing is a natural thing that even the strongest among us feel. Sharing, mutual support, is one of the most beautiful feelings we can have in life. Commitment does not mean life is over. It has just begun.

The flowers on the vine in the school garden have turned a soft velvet-purple. Gorgeous day.

Here we go!
The "we": a Chinese and an American.
Sweet love, I am amazed.

April 28, 1983

I just woke up. It's raining.

May 2, 1983

Spent Labour Day with the Li family. The morning was nice and relaxed. Washed my hair and dried it in the sun, standing on the porch on the second floor. Watched the families walking by, enjoying their vacation together. Most were families of the "one child, two parents" kind. The weather was gorgeous. No one really could have asked for more.

At about quarter past ten, I crowded onto the sardines-packed bus and went to Ruo-xin's house. He had called me earlier that morning and asked if I could come before lunch instead of after. Sure!

We sat and made *jao dz*. I thought about making them for Mom and Dad when we go back to the States.

Alex just came bounding into the room to give me a congratulations hug—Xiao Ming told him yesterday. He was beaming. We talked all about it, he asked the thousand questions everyone asks. How did it happen, does his family know, on and on. He was psyched, sweet boy. The guys all have had positive reactions, compared to Carol, whose feelings were really mixed, and still are. "You're a brave soul with a big heart, Bess," Alex said, smiling, as he left. They all know it will be difficult but well worth it for the sake of love.

The afternoon yesterday was spent at Bei Hai park, sitting on a hill talking about it with Ruo-xin's second eldest brother. He, too, has his reservations, but on the whole has agreed to it. And as far as the difficulties that I can foresee (job, racism, raising children in a mixed Chinese/American fashion in an American society), I have laid them all out quite clearly for him to see. With love, support, and cooperation, there's no difficulty we can't overcome, or at least live through. It has become clear that the number one reason for going to the States rather than staying here is that that is the only way we can spend our lives together. He doesn't think that I could spend my entire life here (and I agree).

The reasons after that are freedom of thought, freedom of personal decision, and so forth. He still believes in socialism and once he gets to know American society I think he will become a true socialist.

Dinner was all of us crowded around the little table. What a feast. Ruo-xin's mother's uncle (seventy-three years old) came from the countryside up north to visit Beijing. He hadn't come for thirty, no thirty-one, years. So what do peasants, workers, and intellectuals (which is what Ruo-xin labeled me) do when they get together for a meal? (1) Turn on the TV. (2) Set up the tape recorder and record their conversation—then play it back and laugh. Particularly amusing is the foreigner's Chinese accent. (3) Eat lots of food. (4) Catch up on stories from the Cultural Revolution.

He, the peasant, ate very little or nothing, lectured to us about the importance of the socialist motto, "Mutual Help" or "Help Each Other," in living and learning. I had taken a nap for an hour before dinner so I felt especially awake and really enjoyed the whole scene. Ruo-xin sat next to me while I slept, and read the paper. When I woke up, we sat and talked about how we wanted to raise our family. It sounds a little stricter than the Spero family, but similar in terms of values and theory. Ruo-xin wants his children to be taught Chinese values which I in my American version also share. But it's not going to be easy, society's influence as the focus of discussion. I told him that even with all our efforts, the kids eventually will decide for themselves and society will be a big factor in their own personal make-up. So it's a gamble.

May 4, 1983

1919—On this day, the students of Beijing rose up in protest against Japan's invasion and against their government's policy. The Twenty-One Demands were unacceptable, so the students cried out and revolution spread. China began on the road to change, the fight against imperialism. Jesus, they were brave, those students.

So my period was two weeks late. I was struck by fear yesterday, so I got a home pregnancy test kit. Fear. Went to the classroom with the intention of not telling Ruo-xin. But of course, I told him. I was really scared. Pictured myself in some alley in Hong Kong getting an abortion.

But I'll tell you, that man of mine. It's not to say he wasn't scared, too. He was. But he took me in his arms, walked around in the soft evening breeze together. "I love you forever, Bessie. Remember, there's no hardship we can't solve."

May 6, 1983   *Friday evening*

You know, I sat down to write and suddenly I can't put the words in order. I have lost my appetite due to my period, which has brought cramps and diarrhea.

Talked to Joey from the hotel this morning. He really sounded excited about the whole thing. I knew he would. The reality of the next two and a half years here hasn't become as much a part of my thoughts as life back in the States has. And even that is difficult to envision. Compared to the initial chaos of feelings, I feel much calmer now. Perhaps I can get back to some serious studying. Or maybe I'll wait until September to go really hard core again.

Lynn, the woman who's in Beijing for research for these next few weeks, made the comment that Ruo-xin is "so young!" Yes, we are, it's true, quite young. What will we be like two years from now? Sometimes I wonder if he ever tries to imagine himself in the States. I know his biggest worry is finding a job. I'm concerned about that, too. But we'll work it out.

Graduation back at Tufts is coming soon. Jesus, college went too fast. And I was too uptight. I wish I could do it over again.

May 8, 1983

Every minute seems like a year long as I wait for Mom and Dad to get the tape telling them that Ruo-xin and I are engaged. I actually almost called them this morning—just to tell them that I've decided to come home for the summer months. But that's crazy. Wait till they get the tape, then call.

Ruo-xin and I went to see the Picasso exhibit at the Fine Arts Museum yesterday afternoon after I got back from visiting the Red Star Commune.

"He's hard to understand," was the basis of most of the comments I heard around me. I've never seen that museum so packed with people. Picasso is a revelation for the Chinese. They seem to appreciate his art simply for its creativity, though, like most human beings who look at a piece of art, they all are trying to extract meaning from his works. I just like to look and let the feelings that emerge wash over my mind and body; if something concrete pops into my senses, well, all the better then for making conversation and sharing feelings.

After Picasso's exhibit, we went to see a collection of photographs done by a Frenchman in the 1940s. The spirited, affectionate, wild characters of the French enchanted the crowds that squeezed together to get a look at the photographs that showed "real life" in another country. They laughed and chattered and stared curiously at the whole room of pictures. I had more fun watching Ruo-xin look at the pictures than looking at anything else.

Our discussion afterwards was out on the benches in front of the museum. The soda was all sold out. We just sat in the shade. The conversation allowed us to forget our thirst; my thoughts wandered to our life together in the States. He patiently accepted my belaboring of this unanswerable topic and we wandered through the questions once more, searching for possibilities. I discovered what he really wanted to be was a doctor. But I didn't ask him why at examination time he didn't take that kind of exam to get into medical school. I'll ask later. He said he'd like to do something in his field, biology, but other fields, like business, would be fine, too. Through the course of conversation the ideal situation, according to him, finally emerged; and this, too, would suit me just fine.

I made the comment that I would perhaps be able to find quite a good job here, he could teach, and we would live very well, even extravagantly according to Chinese standards. He still seems to be convinced that I wouldn't be able to stand living in China. I'm not so convinced of that. I still like it here. Can't anyone understand how I love the feeling of standing in the middle of a (wonderful) human experiment and watching? I know my own country is conducting her own experiment, too. Why not live there? Wherever Ruo-xin is happy, that's where we'll live. I can and will live a happy life in either place. I really believe that. Ruo-xin thinks that with freedom we can live a better life. Maybe so. So the ideal situation as he sees it would be both of us working for a company that sends us to China and back to the United States. Perhaps the majority of the time would be in the U.S. Well, we'll see. That might be hard to find. We could always start our own company. I still want to write that book.

Possibilities. . . . They're endless. Unknown. Scary. We haven't talked to his parents yet, but I think they have an idea. His mother sat down beside me in the bedroom and said, "So where do you want to live, in China or in America?"

I was a little taken aback. She has a question. She asks in all her sweet innocence.

"I'm not sure," I replied.

May 10, 1983   *Tuesday morning, 6:00*

There has been a progressive disillusionment coming over the

Americans here around me. It seemed to begin almost as soon as we got here, and now it's really reached a peak. Sure, there could be a thousand reasons. They could be missing home, having fears about going home and having to look for a job. They perhaps are having a hard time adjusting to such a radically different environment, but even those who are well adjusted seem to be at odds with this place.

"It's so inefficient!"

"This goddamned bureaucracy!"

"The students are too sheltered. They all seem like children," they say condescendingly.

"The food is disgusting."

"The bureaucracy is suffocating us."

Oh, Jesus. My stomach hurts.

You know, the complaining about communication and transportation, logistics—these complaints are somewhat justified. But when they begin to put down the people, there's where the glaring misunderstanding shows up.

"Why don't these people revolt? Don't they know they're in prison?"

That's easy to say when you've never had to fight for your freedom. When you've never felt the pain of starvation and are simply thankful for enough food on the table. When you've never experienced anything like the Cultural Revolution and can't empathize with the relief and desire to tend to your own life now that it's over, now that the neighbors and the local police aren't breathing down your neck.

No one will deny that people are oppressed here, that inequality is evident everywhere you turn. These are things that cannot be denied. But change is slow. And when it comes overnight, then there will be trouble.

The sense of family here is something precious. The camraderie between fellow workers, fellow classmates in particular, and between family members, is true and something to be studied by all other nations.

Sure, some people are disrespectful to one another, often treating foreigners like kings and then treating their own kind like dogs. The point is, when people say, "I'm sick of this place. I can't stand this crazy country," I can't help but think they just haven't opened their eyes to try to understand, they haven't seen enough yet. Or perhaps it's best that they just go home. I, however, can't sit through a dinner with a bunch of griping Americans when there's a world of positive Chinese right outside the door, eating dinner and listening to music over the loudspeakers.

Give me a break; I know the shit about this country. As Jin Hui told me, before the Cultural Revolution there was much more of a dedication to the country by the people. By the people. The government said: we need people to work out in this desolate area. And people went, feeling a sense of obligation to serve the people. But the Cultural Revolution took that precious attitude and crushed it. People are less willing to listen to the government. Want only to tend to their own lives and search for greater comforts. Sure, I know what's shitty about this place. I know how they're like animals when they're pushing to get on the bus.

But I also know their smiles, their hopes. I know their struggles, their fears. I know their loving senses. I know their playfulness in the park. I know the brilliant among them and am astounded at their discipline. I know what they have been through, their disillusionments, and what they are trying to achieve. I see them as human beings, and, as Beth pounded into my head so ruthlessly back in college, I will *not* judge them by my or any standards, but will only extend my hand to them if they are in need, will only try to understand them and appreciate them for what they are.

May 11, 1983

Went to see *Death of a Salesman* tonight. Arthur Miller has been in China directing it for the past month or so.

The obviously most seasoned actor in the play was the most believable. He played Willy Loman. I don't know from what sense memory he pulled the feelings, the confusion, the torment. One might say that the feelings Willy Loman had could be found in a capitalist *or* socialist *or* communist society, as much as the Chinese government would not like us to believe it.

Linda's speech at the end was as true, simple, and profoundly moving as any I've seen. Amazing, coming from actors who were trained in a style in direct contrast to the Stanislavski method that this play was written for. Was it the actors' ability to play so true to life that pulled it off? Is it the innate character of Stanislavski's theory and teachings that makes the method universal? Or is it the play it-self? I'd like to offer that it is all of the above.

God, how I'd love to act again. All I had to do was walk into that theatre and the memories came flooding back. I will always remember that time of my life fondly, as hard as it was—particularly at Tufts.

But you know, I looked at the drained faces of the actors as they took their bows tonight and said to Harry, who was sitting next to me, "I just wouldn't be able to do this play every night—not for over a week, anyway."

I can't help but wonder what these actors went through during the Cultural Revolution. The man who played Willy also translated the play. I understand his English is beautiful, as well.

The set wasn't too complicated, really. A skeleton-frame house with an upstairs bedroom for the parents, center was a neutral area, as was downstage left. Simple enough. At times I glanced at the Chinese around me. They were no less caught up in the life of Willy, Linda, and their sons than I was. They didn't even laugh when the actors cried—which Chinese audiences usually do. I completely forgot about the two hours I had to wait to get my glasses today as I was amazed by not only the courage of these actors to do this play, but also the astounding results of their efforts.

Now there were problems, of course. How to make the flashback scenes believable and at the same time resembling memory-type scenes is difficult for any actor or director to work out. Biff and Happy did not cut the cake. The first half was affected and very far from true to life, in terms of characterization and style. The second half was considerably better.

So Arthur Miller wants us to ask, is Willy Loman's dream worth the cost? How sad for those who think it is. Sweet Ruo-xin, how can I take you back to such a crazy society? I thought about that question during most of the play. I have no answer but to say that Ruo-xin's dream is not Willy Loman's dream, nor is Willy's dream my dream. Ruo-xin and I share a dream of a life together. A simple vision. Willy's hopes for his children? Our hopes are only that they will grow up honest and happy and not scarred by the society that they will have to cope with, but will instead thrive on the freedom that Ruo-xin's classmates will never know. We hope that our love will help them to love themselves, and give them the strength to build their own lives.

Tomorrow I will be twenty-two years old. Life gets better every year. But seriously, can it get any better than the last twenty-one years have been?

And then again, of course it can. The word "possibility" is still at the forefront.

I miss my sweet family tonight. Can't wait to go home again.

It's raining.

Off to sleep.

May 15, 1983   *Sunday afternoon*

Every birthday seems to be better than the one before it. We took off that afternoon and walked around and talked. Hopes for communism, fears of loss of freedom, plans for life in the States, philosophy of how to choose.

Choices. Here in Beijing, I have chosen. Chosen a new route that I had never imagined, never planned on for myself. Judging from my parents' tone of surprise over the phone when I talked to them on Friday, they, too, had had no idea that this was in the cards. Not only has coming to China changed so many of my perspectives (not to speak of all the new questions it has helped me dig up), but the decision to let myself fall in love with a Chinese, a socialist, a biologist: so many characteristics I never thought would exist in the man I would marry. But as Simone de Beauvoir says of herself and Sartre in her book *Force of Circumstances*, which I started on this windy Sunday afternoon, "We believed in socialism as the only way to reach communism." That is perhaps one way to describe Ruo-xin's brand of socialism. He believes the system's strong point is in its people-to-people relationships. And even so, people's relations here are not all that pure and wonderful. I've seen Chinese being shitty to one another quite often.

On another subject, I love the "on the street" court trials. Two people start up an argument on the street and within moments, the two are surrounded by a crowd, a self-selected jury. After listening to as long a testimony as they think is necessary, the crowd intervenes and points to the winner. There is no sentence. Only a decision of who was right, who was wrong. Loss of face by the loser. And then everyone gets bored, disperses, and rides off down the road. Simple as that.

I'm dying to travel again. Traveling home will be great of course, but I really want to get out to western China where the Hans aren't the majority, where the government is far, far away from the people's lives. Patience, my dear.

Back to Bei Hai park. Ruo-xin gave me a photograph album, but the best part about the present was the letter that put his true feelings on paper, a sight my list-oriented, obsessed with "seeing as believing" mind was so happy to see. Not that the thoughts, the hopes, the will, and the love had not already been expressed; but he wrote them beautifully and naturally. I kissed him in broad daylight and then we walked home to a splendid meal cooked by his smiling father, who looked especially happy that evening. Presents of Chinese pajamas and a glass Chinese panda bear that his big brother gave me. We drank wine and even smoked a cigarette after dinner for a special treat. To top it all off, we had a birthday cake, a tradition so foreign to them that they weren't exactly sure how to go about eating it. At first they had it in the center of the table when we sat down to dinner. But the table was so small that there was barely enough room to put the other dishes. So I explained that we could put the cake aside and according to tradition we should eat it after we're done with the meal.

That night we rode the bus back to school, content. Now that I was twenty-two and he twenty-one, I could call him "Little Brother" once again.

Last night, Dianne and Aaron took us to Hou Hai, to a sweet little restaurant that served honeyed lamb as its specialty. We toasted to the future, ate a wonderful dinner, and then walked along the river as the sun set.

I'm already getting anxious about going home for the summer, but I feel even more excited about the thought of returning to Beijing. But then, as I went to get water this afternoon at the water shed, the realization of spending two more years here hit me and I wonder if the two years will seem like fifty.

May 18, 1983

"Wasn't it just yesterday we were wandering wide-eyed through Canton?" someone asked as we rolled along on the bus to the final banquet for the foreign students of the university.

I look at Professor Wang, good old "Blinky"—must be nervous today. He was blinking away furiously, smiling, chewing some gum that Carol's parents had brought from the U.S. The banquet actually was quite nice, I sat next to the geography professor and Professor An. I remember the first day we met. I was wearing the same blouse. I remember her smile, her round face.

Professor Zheng came up to me afterwards and said to me quietly, "We should congratulate you tonight, too, Bai Yu-sha."

"Thank you. None of the other professors know. We can leave it that way for now." Rhoda is signing her final papers tomorrow. She is to marry a Chinese student from here, as well. And it wasn't easy—the red tape, the screaming, the wondering, the waiting for all the departments to approve all the thousands of things.

"Is it the right thing to do?" I dare to ask myself. I have to believe in what I feel is right. I can't lead my life any other way.

As we sat on the park bench tonight, we talked over the theories on Lin Biao's death and my Chinese roommate's reaction to the Lin Biao article in *Newsweek*. She reads English fairly well, and translated most of it herself. I helped with the slang. But even though she had come upon a "new" (to the average Chinese citizen, new; to us, not a new theory) way of looking at Lin Biao's apparent plane crash over the Soviet Union, she said herself it wasn't the kind of thing she would discuss with her classmates.

"Most of us are like that," Ruo-xin said. "We don't have any direct relationship with the government. If they deceive us, we don't know. And even if a few did know, it would be crazy to risk your neck over it. Besides, Mao's government is not the Chinese government of today."

I recall sitting in the classroom when we were having a discussion about what a free democracy is and whether or not it exists in China. A people that has no relationship with its government—that is not a democracy. It goes without saying, as Mom mentioned on the tape today, that democracy is a mixed blessing. But I'd still rather have the struggle that comes along with democracy than the mind control of socialism. After sitting deep in thought for a while, my classmates said slowly: No, we have no democracy here. It's all a farce, a fake.

I don't know if I'd be able to live with that. But he has no choice, sweet boy, such a bright human being who feels trapped here. Ruo-xin, who never had a real burning desire to leave in the first place, has the opportunity to leave. But this classmate of his (and many others like him, I'm sure) has no way out. He understands too well, sees too clearly—and will forever long to leave.

May 20, 1983   *Joey's birthday*

Peter's letter came a few days ago, filled with support and love. We stood in front of the men's dorm and I translated the letter to Ruo-xin. We both wanted to cry, feeling so relieved and happy that Pete and Sal were glad about Ruo-xin joining the family.

Got Dad's letter this morning before the banquet. Compared to the phone conversation, which was predictably vague and confusing, and did not hold the same tone as the letter. What a wonderful letter. It was positive, objective, constructive. Amen. Their questions all have answers, for the most part. That's one of the important reasons to go home, to explain the details to them, fill in as many gaps as I possibly can. I can't wait to see them all. Still, I've walked around numb for the past two days. Not knowing what to feel, only because I feel so much right now. Can't bear the thought of leaving China when it feels like I just got here, and at the same time can't wait to get home, to land at O'Hare Airport and feel the ground of the good ole U.S.A., once more. To sit around with my family on the porch, listen to Studs Terkel in the afternoon, and watch Chicago's June go by.

Got the first cold I've had in months this week. Ugh! To top it off, we all got drunk at our last banquet with the faculty this afternoon. Our fearless leader, Professor Shu, really got off on toasting to my engagement. Toast after toast, as we slowly drank ourselves into a sauced oblivion. I found my way back to my bed as soon as the whole thing was through, and slept for three hours.

Woke up and continued reading the article in the *Atlantic Monthly* that Cathy sent me about Murry Flashbeck, the eternal student of the Soviet Union who had done so much in helping us to understand the U.S.S.R. Daddy talked about the necessity to go to graduate school. If we can afford it, I really do want to go; I'm just not sure if it's worth the price. For personal satisfaction—I'd love it. But would it really help me to get a better job? It's hard to say. But reading this article makes me want to go all the more. There is a need. I want to help fill it.

This is a possibility that Ruo-xin and I have been talking about: When we get back to the States, he'll take a year strictly for studying English. During that year, I'll work and apply to grad schools. Once I find out where (if) I'm accepted, we'll move to the location of the graduate school where I'll start the grad program and he'll start technical school in order to train to be a lab technician. Perhaps that's cutting it a little close—maybe he'll need two years of just English study—but I don't think so. So I probably will be about twenty-six by the time I start grad school, if I go at all. That sounds fine to me. Ruo-xin really is itching to get going and start working, be it in the U.S. or China, but he realizes the necessity of getting training in the U.S. This plan hopefully will lay a good base so that we can avoid the very real fear Daddy wrote of in the letter of being forty-three years old with three kids and an unemployed husband. I think if we work hard and play our cards right, we'll avoid that outcome.

May 22, 1983

I leave tomorrow for the States. Home!

My last evening at school was, as it should have been, spent with friends. After dinner I sat with Yin Zi and a few of her gang on the rehearsal stage. The school "leadership" had just recently forbidden them to put on a play that they had been preparing for months, about the life and times of a university student.

"There's nothing we can do about it," they said to me.

"They don't understand the play so they won't let us put it on, that's all."

But tonight they had their noses to the grindstone once more and were preparing to rehearse a new play. These people are amazing.

Went to the biology department classroom to find Wu Xiao Ping to chat and say goodbye. She had come by earlier while I wasn't around. She, like Ruo-xin, doesn't think I should bring the book, banned here on the mainland, that my friend requested from Taiwan. I just don't know what to think. There are so many ways to approach this question. The prevalant fear in the Central Party seems to be that naive Chinese youth, burning with the heat of life's fire, will try to imitate the people they read about if exposed to pornographic literature. Or if exposed to pornographic songs, they will be similarly influenced.

But don't they understand? The government is telling them, dictating to them what they can and cannot think. Is right and wrong defined in terms of government policy? I could scream. From literature to philosophy to music, people should have the right to choose.

"But young people don't know any better. They'll spend their whole time listening to rock music, reading porno novels, and screwing in the bushes," some Chinese have said to me—including my dearly beloved Ruo-xin.

But freedom! What about the freedom of thought and mind? Obviously, he came to his unanswerable problem before I brought it up. He, Xiao Ping, and the others don't have an answer.

"You can't let freedom, pornography, etc., run loose in a country that hasn't been exposed to these things before. People don't know how to handle it. It's not like you, who have grown up with all this input. The Chinese have not. The government has to treat them differently," Ruo-xin said.

"Economics: In terms of development, freedom is the name of the game. In terms of societal ethics, interpersonal relations and thoughts—these things must be carefully protected and the evil must be stamped out," it has been said to me.

I just don't know.

So at lunch today, a classmate (from a province down south; I'm just getting used to his accent) told me that in English class today they started to learn the song "The Sounds of Silence." I thought of Uncle Dick and wished that I could write to him, share with him these new thoughts and experiences. I can just see him coming over to China, just to have a look around. It's strange, the times when I really realize that he's dead. Anyway, I thought that was great that they were learning that song. I explained why I thought the meaning of the song was so important for his country right now. "Silence like a cancer grows," the song says. They must speak up. There are changes socially and politically that are just about to emerge, but will only do so if they cease their passivity, if they end this silent acceptance of social and political oppression.

What made them accept this system for so long? I think back to the lecture my geography teacher gave yesterday. She was talking about her life as a fifteen-year-old girl in Shanghai in 1947. Beggars in the street. People selling their children. Walking to school on the cold winter mornings and passing frozen bundles, babies left outside to die because there was no food to give them. And of course, it was even worse in the countryside. Slowly the standard of living rose after the Communists took over. Although the Cultural Revolution held their development back significantly, great improvements have been made since 1976. Everyone has food and clothing. Going from nothing on the table and no clothes but what they wore on their backs, to what they have today, is enough to make the most thankless person thankful. "It's so much better than it was before," I'm told over and over again. So, they accept, silently, the bad that comes along with the good. Anything is better than what they had before. But now there is a new generation, actually two new generations who don't know what it was like to suffer, who don't have the comparative perspective that makes accepting the present flaws easier. They are the ones who have the new ideas. They want to dance (which is illegal, except for waltzing and such), they want to study what they choose, they don't want to go to these damn, boring political meetings that every homemaker, student, and worker attends once every week. But still, even these young people remain silent.

"Make your opinion known," I've said to nearly every one of my acquaintances here. "Everyone, together, en masse, stop going to the Friday political meetings. Don't be passive," I tell them. "This is your country, and it should be run how you want it to be run." Ah, yes, so easy to say. What if I were in their position? And in certain sense, aren't I in a similar position relative to my own good and society? Aren't there certain changes that need to be made? What am I doing about those things? Change: it's risky, it's slow, it's trying the untried. Who has the courage? I'm looking to my Chinese comrades of my generation to take on the task.

And I don't know what to do about the book. Most of all I don't want to get caught red-handed bringing into the country a book that has been banned from publication. But it's the principle of freedom I'm trying to defend. Don't actions speak louder than words? After chatting a while, Ruo-xin came and sat next to us and read the paper. He and his buddy went out for a walk.

"Want to go out for a bit?"

"No thanks, we'll come out later," I called after him. Xiao Ping and I laughed ourselves silly.

Later on we did go out into the fresh night air, strolled around. Bumped into himself and then the three of us went to the flower garden to smell the flowers. Such sweet smells! A fight broke out in front of the building, people were hanging out of the windows yelling.

We wandered our way back to the flower garden and the benches. And suddenly, something very out of the ordinary came into view. I'm sure I wasn't hallucinating. Ruo-xin saw it, too. We just stood and watched. Smiled. About eight students had set the tape recorder outside and in the shadows, stood around smoking cigarettes and dancing to American songs (waltzing, too) "Five Hundred Miles," etc. Slender, graceful figures waltzed underneath the vines. A precious moment.

We walked back to the dorm and said good night. We had spent a wonderful afternoon together on this cloudy day. And now, time to sleep.

I want to mention the lecture that Ruo-xin's professor gave their class recently. In a lecture evaluating the "Culture and Politeness" month, he mentioned how they needed to conserve electricity a bit better and not waste so much rice. And with regard to foreigners the professor warned: Be on guard. The newspaper has announced incidents of finding spies here on the Mainland—but there are many that are not announced. Be careful in your relationships with foreigners. Be on the lookout.

In other words: Let's make everyone a bit more paranoid so they're just that much more willing to listen to and obey orders from higher up. Ruo-xin was being singled out in the blaring subtext.

It's scary.

It's frustrating.

And it doesn't look like this kind of behavior is being stamped out.

Ugh!

May 24, 1983   *Morning 6:00*
   On the train to Canton

I'm lying here in the upper berth of the sleeping car, train number 47, headed south. Outside it's raining, crying the tears I was brave enough not to shed yesterday when I said goodbye to Ruo-xin and his family at the train station. All around me are Hong Kong Chinese, yapping away in their singsonglike dialect.

The music just came on over the loudspeakers. Soft, sweet wake-up music. Then the reminder to keep the train clean, conserve water, and respect your fellow travelers. Also to say that we're passing the Henan province.

Wasn't it just yesterday that I was riding this train for the first time up to Beijing in the hot days of August?

Last night was rather uncomfortable until I finally fell asleep. My lungs are all screwed up from this cold, so every time I lay down to go to sleep I can't breath. A rather frustrating experience. Somehow it cleared up a bit and I fell asleep. Why is it that every time I get set to travel I get sick?

Rested at Ruo-xin's yesterday afternoon and then ate a good dinner with them. Ruo-xin and I spent a few hours in the afternoon in the outer room, talking. Mostly about speaking out and how change happens in China today. After dinner we loaded up and he and his brothers took me to the train station. A moment not to be forgotten, all four of us standing on the bus. Looking at their smiling faces. As we stood in line at the train station, I felt someone tap my shoulder. It was Ruo-xin's father.

"You forgot your medicine! Here, I brought it for you.... It doesn't matter," he said. "I'm not busy." He smiled from ear to ear.

And before I knew it, the train was rolling out of the station. Goodbye, Beijing, Goodbye, sweet Li family. I'm waiting until I can be with you again.

It was an amazing year.

May 25, 1983

Well, wouldn't you know it. Here we are, just an hour away from Canton. I am awakened from a peaceful sleep by the cleaning woman who wants to make the bed and urges me to get my things ready. OK. No problem.

Suddenly, the train lurches to a stop in the middle of a tropical forest. Not unusual, really. Maybe we ran over another peasant or maybe there's an ox blocking the tracks. I get out my fan to keep off the mosquitoes that are having breakfast on the flesh of the unannounced guests in their forest. All the men around me are spitting and coughing and smoking. Ah yes, a pleasant way to spend the morning. Finally, the word makes it back to our car: something needs repair. Delay: three hours. Well, there goes my chances of making it to Hong Kong today. Ugh! I could scream. If only I hadn't lost my voice, I'd be able to chat with the people around me. Frustration. My cough is coming from deep in my chest. Where is there any air to breathe?

Later that night

Finally made it to Canton. It hardly seems like China, what with all the fancy hotels, delicious food, and aggressive men and women. Every time I go traveling in China it hits me clear as a bell: China is made up of many different worlds.

I've come to a conclusion after a year of traveling: I really would prefer not to travel by myself. Traveling is really a pleasure when there's someone there to share the sights and sounds. In my passion to prove my independence, I have always declared in the past that I love to travel alone. But as I realize now (now that I can make a comparison of what it's like to travel with someone versus alone), that when I'm with a friend, I have much more courage, and explore much deeper into the places I go to. Whereas when I travel by myself, I lose my courage, tend to stick close to the familiar, well-traveled paths—and in general feel just less excited about the trip.

I will not call this a loss of independence. Instead, I will call it a recognition of my real feelings coming to the surface and will welcome them on the basis that they are honest, human, and subject to change.

Now that I've said that—Ugh! I can't wait to get home!

May 28, 1983

Here's hoping I'll get a plane out of here this morning.

That's not to say Hong Kong hasn't been wonderful. Overlooking the fact that I haven't been able to sleep much at night, walking around Hong Kong's streets, dinner in her Bostonlike bars, watching the fog lift from Victoria Peak—the place is really a world in itself. I can't help but wonder what Ruo-xin will feel when we come here two years from now.

Hong Kong, the final stop before lift off to the Western world. This is an appropriate place to end this volume, seeing as how I started it on my journey to Asia. Just right; I can end it on my way home. I hope the next journals will be better than this, more informative, less X-rated. There's always hope for improvement. Time to pack this book into my suitcase.

Affectionately yours,

Bessie A. Spero

Part II

探 家

A Visit Home
Summer 1983

June 5, 1983

Back in the Western world, my home. Back again with my family, my amazing family. I am so happy to be here. There's only one thing that's bothering me and that is that Ruo-xin hasn't written yet. Or his letter hasn't arrived, anyway. I've written him three times already. Once from Canton, twice from the U.S. God, I hope nothing's happened to him. I have to admit, a part of me (the irrational side that Brian always complained about) fears the worst. If they did anything to him—well, I'll raise hell, that's for sure. I'll publish every scathing detail I know about that goddamned government. If only he would just send word that all is well. I miss you, sweetest love of my life. I miss you.

Everywhere I go, everything I see, I think, "How will this look to him?" He'll be amazed. I'm amazed myself. I never realized what luxury and comfort we live in.

The cars, the road. The grocery store. So clean and full of anything your heart desires. The kitchen alone flips me out compared to what I've lived with the past eight months. All conveniences, the appliances, the plastic bags, the frig. The carpets, the furniture. The clothing. I have so much clothing. It's embarrassing.

And most of all, the space. We have space here. Private space. Clean air floats among the leaves on the the trees that stand in the yard, a huge space compared to the crowded city of Beijing.

And the people here. That's a flip out. So affectionate, outgoing. Clothing so colorful.

Went to see *Return of the Jedi* tonight with my brother Peter, and my cousins Lisa and Carol. Just the sound system in that theatre alone is enough to astound you, after spending the last year in rundown theatres in China, run by ancient technology. The Japanese film I saw was good, though. Still, I can't wait for the day when I can sit in the Highland Park Edens Theatre and watch a movie with Ruo-xin. It's a dream. A dream, but in two years please, it's got to come true. It's just got to.

I do feel different than when I left here last August. More patient, I guess. Less hurried, less worried. I wonder what did it. Probably a thousand different factors.

All I can say is, it's a relief. I really would feel better though if Ruo-xin's letter would get here. Perhaps it will come tomorrow. My sweet family has fallen in love with him already, After hours of talking, sorting out, thinking, planning, questioning, considering, together we have all gone over every point from the easiest to the most sensitive topics. It's all out in the open and our mutual support is stronger than ever. I do love this family of mine.

June 10, 1983

It's true, coming home has helped me sort a few things out, see things a bit more clearly. The response from Anexter Brothers Corporation was surprising, but gave me a clue into how valuable my qualifications and background may be. If only I'd taken calculus and accounting, though! Studs Terkel's immediate enthusiasm about setting up an interview to make a tape of my eight months in China was encouraging, too. I just didn't expect all this response. And, of course, I'm thrilled about it. Jesus, who wouldn't be. I just hope Ruo-xin has a positive reaction to all this. I hope that it isn't just empty talk when he says he supports me in my career. He doesn't really realize what that means.

June 13, 1983

It's funny, but the problem of nuclear power's waste products and where to put them has come back to slap me in the face once again. I guess I sort of forgot about it. But I heard on National Public Radio today that they want to put a low-level nuclear waste site here in Illinois. Jesus.

On the brighter side of things. The house smells the same, smells like home. The stairs still creak the same as ever. But my bed. My bed is more comfortable than ever.

Spent the day making phone calls (University of Chicago, First National Bank, Educational Testing Service, on and on) and got the porch back together. Scrubbed down the walls, the glass, cleaned the floor with the radio on. Sweated. Read *The New York Times*. What a pleasure. And now that my résumé is out and the responses have come in, options arise and life seems to hold more possibilities than ever before. Living it with my family is the greatest joy I have. Once Ruo-xin is here, then it'll be complete. As long as I have my career as well, I'll be OK.

The media. The news. Radio, TV, newspapers—amazing. Sure, I know they shovel the shit at times and are out to make a buck. But

still, we *get* the *news*. A vast array of subjects, differing opinions, stories of all kinds. It's really exciting and informative. I can't wait until
Ruo-xin can hear and understand it, too. Will it ever happen? I so believe it will. And yet, there is an iota of fear. Never mind. We'll pull it
off.

Mom and Dad are exhausted after a long, busy day of work. But
happily tired. It's better than being bored.

Sal spent the afternoon in the yard with us yesterday. We talked
about China, reminisced about how seven years ago at this time she
and Pete were falling in love. Speaking of that time, I never jotted
down how good it was to see Peter Drew and the rest of the Evanston
crowd last week. George and Barry drove me back to Highland Park
one last time. They're heading out west. Pete's coming back, though,
in July.

Christ, time flies by.

Speaking of which, I went outside to pick up the mail and what
was there? A wedding invitation to Christian and Christine's wedding. In France. Take me back, huh. The basement rooms in Carpen-
ter House. David. Beth's smile. Brian's songs. Don's office. Christian.
Sweet Christian.

Enough of this sentimentality. God, just the entertainment
around here is astounding. The color, the technology, the imagina-
tion. People who know how to play, to live, to love, to work—these
things my country does well. Too bad we don't have an equally
matching President. Our foreign policy is in shambles due to his lack
of tact and understanding. It will take years to patch up the breaks
he's caused not only with the Soviets, but in the Western alliance itself.

I wonder what Cathy finally ended up doing in Costa Rica? I
can't wait to get her next letter.

Democracy. Real freedom. It has its price; the bad ideas are allowed to emerge, too, if they can make it. The good and the bad. All
are open to scrutiny, to support, or to criticism. It's just frustrating
when the crap comes into control.

Lawrence just called—to talk to Mom. The first friends, along
with Sylvie Meyer, who have expressed real disapproval over the
marriage. Actually, Sylvie went on a rampage. Lawrence's wish just
remained silent. A screaming silence.

Go to hell. I'll forgive. When we're married, when it's all settled and they see how well it works out—they'll accept it, and I'll forgive. But their shit right now is just plain disappointing. I guess this is a battle we'll fight forever. It's just a beginning.

June 14, 1983

Looks like a storm is coming our way tonight. Saw it off in the distance as I stood in front of Daddy's office in Highland Park this afternoon. Now it's just about to start.

I guess I'm obsessed with the media these days. Really, ever since I got back, I've just been amazed at the flood of information that flows out of the radio, TV, and newspapers into our homes and offices. Heard on National Public Radio today that the Chileans have had enough of their latest regime, which has been in power for ten years now. The whole country protested today and the pot may blow its lid soon. Those poor people. Consistent with Chile's history, the protesters will be "taken care of" one by one or in mass quantities. Christ, they are brave, those people. As the Chinese man in the restaurant remarked to me earlier this afternoon, "People here in the U.S. just don't appreciate the freedoms they have."

I finally have come to the realistic conclusion that living with anyone isn't easy, be it friend, lover, or parent. But there is something that makes it easier and that's acceptance. Acceptance that everyone has his or her own little quirks, own sensitivities, limits, boiling points, one different from the next. If one can just accept those differences and make the goal "Let's all live together, accept one another, and try our best to make one another comfortable, or at the very least just let everyone run his or her own life," then the situation is a workable one. It calls for sacrifice, it leaves little or no room for laziness, it calls for a positive attitude and a sensitivity for others.

I wonder if it was living in China that made me come to that realization, watching how well they deal with one another in such overcrowded, not necessarily the most desirable living conditions (usually, though certainly not always—for example, street fights and arguments on the bus). Or was it just something that happens when one grows a year older?

June 18, 1983

Cousin Bob and Aunt Shirley came into Chicago Friday—for Bob's graduation today. It was a gorgeous day, by the way, for a graduation. I'll bet it would have been great at Tufts. As much as I try not to think about it, I feel just awful that I missed Tufts graduation. I just didn't plan ahead for it. Now I wish I had gone. Ah, well, water under the bridge. Gorgeous green lawn in front of Ballou Hall. Remember freshman year. God, the memories come flooding back as I lie here in my bed on Oakland Drive. Sweet times, sad times, amazing that it really was my life.

I'm sorry Uncle Larry couldn't see Bobby graduate. But we were there. And Aunt Shirley did quite well.

My mind is drifting. I guess it's because the radio's on. I wanted to write about Bob's party Friday night and the lobsters he brought, and his friends. About the blue sky today. About Daddy. But I just am not in the mood. I put it out of my mind for the most part. But thoughts of the next few years are constantly on my mind.

I called Nathan in Washington this morning. He was asleep. I guess I just wanted to touch base with something in the past. I don't know why.

June 19, 1983

Nathan called tonight. Somehow I knew he'd return my call. He sounds just the same, but happier. There's somebody with a direction, career-wise anyway. I only hope he can find his love, as I have found mine. I tried to help him find it in me; but now that I've come to know Ruo-xin, I realize how mismatched Nathan and I were. Still, it's a good friendship. He's making a big salary this summer so he's flying to Boston to see me when I head out that way in July. I'll see Cathy in August and then my trip will be complete, and I can head back to China.

If it weren't for a few loose ends around here, I'd love to go back to Beijing tomorrow. There's something so refreshing about living in a totally different society. It's exciting, fascinating, frustrating—all at once. I want to be on my bicycle, riding down the main drag of the city. I want to be back in the dorm, studying Chinese. I want to go back and watch the country at work and at play. I want to see Xio Ming and Yin Zi. And most of all, I want to see Ruo-xin. The thrill of being home is wearing off. I miss him more and more. I'm itching to talk to him. There's so much to talk about and I have a terrible time trying to put it into a letter in Chinese. Bobby said to me yesterday, "Gee, it must be hard for you. I mean, your fiancé is in Beijing." You know, I never thought of it as being something difficult. And it isn't.

But there's something, a part of me, maybe, that's there with him.

I'm looking forward to seeing Liu Mei-chun and meeting her husband. God, I hope I can still carry on a conversation in Chinese. I'm afraid I'm forgetting so much.

I know my meetings in Boston won't produce miracles, but I at least hope that talks with Professors Terry and Klein will bring to light some attractive ideas. I'd feel better if I went back to China with some idea of what I'm heading for once I get back to the U.S. But that may be too much to ask.

June 20, 1983

What will I finally choose as a career for this life? Or at least, where will I begin?

I see a program on TV about the First Amendment and the press and I suddenly want to be a journalist. I want to inform, keep the public aware.

Or work on policy making. A think tank type of operation.

Or a presidential advisor on the Far East and the Soviet Union.

Or a trial lawyer.

Or become an expert on American business and management and teach the Chinese what they're itching to know.

Or become a professor of political science or foreign policy.

Let's talk about it later.

June 27, 1983

Joey leaves tomorrow to return to New York. We hadn't seen each other for a year. So much is happening in our lives, so much that we could share with each other. And beyond that, I really need his help in talking about career ideas. But these past four days, in between the sunshine, sitting by the pool, looking at slides, going out for dinner and listening to Michael Jackson, we didn't share a word of any of the important things. That's not to say it wasn't a joy having him here. I enjoy his company. Period. Whether we speak or not. But, as it has been for all twenty-two years of our relationship, there is a mountain of words, a sea of interactions that we never shared. I wish I knew why. Maybe it is my fault, maybe it's not. But that's not the point. I used to try—to probe, to ask questions, get things started. But he only answered and then left it at that. He never took the ball and ran with it. I always felt as if I were pushing, forcing us down the avenues of a conversation. And although I tried a bit this time, too, I tried a little less. Once I saw the same pattern occurring again, I gave up. The wall is too high for me.

Maybe he sees this as the way things ought to be. "Who needs to say all the details?" I can hear him saying. "Isn't silent communication enough?"

No, it never was for me. An empty space. A part of me that is dying to share with him. It hurts.

I know, or I think I know, that it's not that he's not interested. Maybe he's just caught up with his own life. Maybe he doesn't feel comfortable taking the ball and running . So I should just accept it as it is, a loving relationship.

Isn't it ridiculous? I wanted more than that. I wanted to share ideas and experiences and guidance and dreams. But it just never happened. And there's nothing I can do about it. Why should I want more than love?

I'm itching to show him this journal entry; maybe it would help. But then again, maybe it would only hurt him. And the last thing I want to do is make him feel sad. I've never been one who gave up easily. But after twenty-two years I think this situation is one I'd better come to accept.

The letter from Ruo-xin Saturday. I never thought being so far away would be so hard. We have a lifetime; two months is no great shakes. Actually, a good time for personal exploration. But when the communication lines seem to be broken, then I can feel every inch of those twelve thousand miles. He wrote June 10 that he hadn't gotten a letter since I wrote to him from Canton. I can't imagine that none of my letters reached him. No way to answer the question, "Why?" And no quick way to comfort his worried mind. I sent a letter to Reeva in Beijing, asking her to go find him and let him know that I in fact have written three letters since Canton, have received all of his, that my family welcomes him (though they have fears about his adjustment here) and that I'm not going to Taiwan. If I don't hear from either of them soon, I'll send a telegram.

I think we'd better get used to this. But Christ, will he even understand why I have to be back in the States a year from now to start graduate school while he finishes college in Beijing? I hope so. There really is no other way.

I'm looking forward to going out to Boston in July. It'll be good to see old friends again.

July 3, 1983

Mom and Dad's thirty-second anniversary. We sat on the porch this morning. Talked about careers, revisionist history, our ancestors. Called Gram and she told me about her days as a child, Uncle Al, and Great Grandma Sax's divorce and her arranged marriage. Sleeping on kitchen chairs when she lived with her poor relatives while Great Grandma Sax had T.B. Great Grandpa's escape from Latvia during the Prussian War. Such hard lives. Survivors. I wonder how far Ruo-xin has delved into his past, the lives of his ancestors? My mind reaches back to Latvia, Ellis Island, Great Grandpa's house in Russia, places I've never been.

Called Liu Mei-chun at Tufts this morning. So good to hear her voice. Mom and Dad asked if she knew about Ruo-xin. I think they do, she and her husband. She's read all my letters to Cathy, so she must know. I'll have to ask Cathy in a letter. I don't think they would try to stop it. If anything, they would do what they could to help, I think. But then, who knows?

I guess I've got to be careful. Jesus, if this whole thing works out, it'll be a miracle. But I know it will come to be. It has to. And it's not just a hope, the Chinese constitution is on our side, protecting our right to marry—that is, if they don't change it next year.

Peter Drew came home from Oregon a few days ago. There's another amazing happening in my life. That we have been able to turn a strong love, a deep hurt, into a friendship that means so much to both of us. These are the things that make my life worth living.

July 6, 1983

My mind is dizzy with thoughts. Talk about unexpected. The Tufts yearbook came today. The world stopped, I sat down at the kitchen table and read the whole thing. A book of memories, friends, a time that seems a blur to me today. I wish I could do it all over again. I could get so much more out of it now. But it was an amazing three years.

The sky is so damned blue today. My mind has been filled with thoughts of the U.S.A. these days. And what it looks like to an immigrant. What is their struggle like? How will Ruo-xin feel here? Will he ever come to love this country? Will his children? Or will they go back to China?

July 4th—Saturday on the lawn of Northwestern University campus with Peter Drew and Joe Bushman. Watched the fireworks. Joked and laughed. Pondered our lives here. Wandered what it was like to be a revolutionary in 1776? What was it like to win?

Later, weaving through the crowds of Evanston folks, all shapes, colors, and sizes. People were living it up. We made our way to 31-flavors, Pete had a malt, and I had a root beer float. Walked along the old turf, sharing a once again new plane of communication. Reveling in the feeling of freedom and the time to be able to share time together again. Hold my hand. You forgave me, I forgave you. Laugh with me. Remember this park? What do you think? Go for it. Acceptance.

I'll always be here for you.

Be strong. Let's make our dreams come true. I'll be there for you when when they come alive, and when they crumble.

Coffee.

Drove down Green Bay Road at two in the morning for the eighty millionth time. I love you, Peter Drew.

Got to get ready for work.

Ruo-xin's letter says my letters are getting through now. I hope we're doing the right thing. What would my life be without him? I don't know. I just pray he can be happy here. I just pray.

July 17, 1983   *At the Cape*

I never knew coming back to visit old friends could be so wonderful. I woke up this morning on Cape Cod at David's house. Heaven.

Coming to Boston has been a flip just in itself. Such a gorgeous city, I mean just in terms of buildings, architecture, streets. And so colorful. Every kind of person you could imagine is here, from the African drum players in the park in Cambridge to the punk rockers in the square to the preppie. Young, old, and in between from all corners of the earth have come here to live or go to school. I love it. I can just imagine Ruo-xin's face when he sees all this.

Cousin Bob and I went to the North End to Regina's for pizza the first night I got in. What a treat. Sweet cousin of mine. We watched the Italian parade pass by the door of the restaurant. A whole group of Italians marched behind whoever the saint was that was being celebrated. They sang and the little band played a song from the old country. Tears filled the eyes of a few as they were transported back to their homeland, Italy, sent back on the words of the song. And the parade marched on, they passed by, walking together.

The pizza was great and being with Bob again was as much a pleasure as it always is. Transition time right now, for both of us. Neither of us can really imagine what life will be like a year from now; it's nice to have each other.

Time to go downstairs—*déjà vu*. Two years ago—Michael, Willy, Mooney, David, Christian, Christine. That was a riot of a time we spent out here. Michael told me in the car last night on the way home from the airport that Willy's father died last year. Jesus. And Christian is married now. Time is flying by. I intend to finish the events of the weekend later. This is a time to remember.

July 18, 1983

Morning, Monday. Back at Bob's apartment after a jam-packed three days. Being back in Boston; so good to be with old friends again, so hard to say goodbye—again—so soon after we'd just said hello.

I waited for Nathan at the airport. Nervous. Excited. He came out of the gate, tall, the same good-looking man I left over a year ago. But over the course of the next twenty-four hours that we spent together, it was clearer that he's a much happier soul than he was a year ago. We made our way into Cambridge, so amazed to be seeing each other again. Grinning like zanies. Sat in Uno's and drank Piña Coladas, looked at pictures of China, shared the year. Talked about the "differences" question in a relationship. Although he and I had a lot of them, he's afraid Ruo-xin and I will have too may differences. Politically, socially, even intellectually, in terms of family, and last but not least, we see the world as our home, not just the U.S. In terms of all these things, Ruo-xin and I have more in common than Nathan and I do.

Still, Nathan and I share to this day, a fascination with each other's differences and a joy in the intellectual stimulation that comes in our interaction with each other. Like the best of loves, we appreciate each other for better or worse.

Stayed at Bob's last night. We finally fell asleep at two-thirty that morning, woke up at nine o'clock to a gorgeous, sunny Boston day. Nathan and I wandered around Cambridge, went to the law school, and then the International Law Journal office, where we spent a good portion of the afternoon. There's so much fabulous reading material in that place, I could have spent all day there.

We indulged in our favorite thing, discussions on ethics, international relations, personal relationships, our goals, dreams. Nathan got a lot off his chest. Watching me discover the world, he says, makes him feel like an old fogie—set in his lifestyle, unadventurous.

I told him that whatever came naturally, whatever made him happy (and that probably includes doing something worthwhile for the cause of human rights, nuclear power, and the law of the international community) was what he should be doing.

To touch base again has done me a lot of good. Reassurance that old friends are here, stronger than ever, life is still going on, even though I am zipping off to far corners of the earth where I live as a stranger for nine months. It's a good reassurance to come back to old friends again.

Sat by the banks of the Charles where he walked this fall, wondering what it would have been like if I hadn't gone away. (Thank God I went away.)

Finally I met Thai. We went out for dinner with him that night. Nationalist, wide-faced Korean boy, educated at Yale undergrad and then at Harvard law school. Talked about the Asian concept of marriage in contrast to the very me-oriented, career number one, family number two, type of marriage for many Americans. The Asians believe, as the Speros do, that love means you're happy when the other person is. Family is number one, not to be sacrificed for one's career. This concept woven with the idea of a partnership, both male and female doing their crucial part to make the show go on, is universal. Talked about career. What to choose. They both encouraged the private sector, even though Thai is heading for the public sector. "You'll be appreciated in the private sector," they urged me.

I have a feeling people are overestimating the importance of my knowledge of Chinese.

The Contadora Group called for an end to foreign interference in Central America. Please listen, Mr. President, please listen.

Maybe it's teaching where I can make the most difference. I love the academic atmosphere. I'll call Daddy. Just let him know all is well and to hear his voice.

My stomach went on the blink again. They drove me over to College Avenue, the home of my favorite "slum lords." I can't believe Willy's father is dead. And Winky. As we sat around the table at the Cape, Beth told me that Winky was killed in New York City. That's just too hard to take. Sweet Winky. Dead. God will damn that city—if he hasn't already.

As we stood on the porch at College Avenue and Jim Marcus told me the story of Christian and Christine's marriage at the real estate agent's office, Brian drove up. He was easier to communicate with than I've felt in a long time. And still just as spirited as ever. Nathan decided that he and Thai would get on their way. So good to have seen Nathan, even if it was for just a short time. It was heavenly. That friendship will never die.

We hopped in the car and drove out to the Cape. Blasted Pat Metheny, American Garage over the stereo. Heaven. As we drove along, we listened to Brian's new music, which I love, though I miss the folk music. And Jim and Pam caught me up on the lives of all our classmates. Some actually have found jobs, others have not. All the engineers, needless to say, are employed. No one was taking off to strange places all over the earth—except me.

Drove up to Hyannis and Dave's house. Beth came running out of the house; a year was enough time to repair old wounds. Love survives. That night and the next day we packed. We went skinny dipping in the ocean that night, they couldn't help themselves but to launch into a million questions about China. Slept so well that night.

The next day was pancake breakfast and then off to the beach. We sailed and I sat on the sand. Out on the boat with Michael and David, they recounted the story of the student takeover of the Tufts administration building last year in protest of the Professor Drier issue and the tenure problem. Amazing.

Talk has become more realistic than ever about work and families. To be expected. Funny. The one of the group who had direction for so long, me, has totally lost direction and is now up in the air. "When we heard that," Michael said, "we thought the end had come, our last hopes disappeared." But spending time together, it's clear that each one will find his or her way, in due time. I think most of us felt reassured by our meeting together.

Beth looks more wonderful than ever, even with Winky's death. Jesus, every spring something happens. In 1982 it was Leila and Mrs. Newman, and Uncle Larry in fall 1981, and then in 1983 it was Winky. It's hardest when we have to see our friends die.

Saw slides of China that night—they loved it. Everyone thinks I should share these experiences with institutions, universities, the public. I guess at least I should write some articles. But I'm afraid to do that, for fear of jeopardizing my marriage with Ruo-xin. Maybe I'll write some while I'm in China next year. We'll see.

Although brief, it was a precious time I spent with them. I'll never forget all of us on the beach together, sitting on the blanket and sharing our thoughts, lives, jokes, sweet times.

The weekend has renewed some of my faith, as much of this summer has, in my classmates. Human beings, trying to find a corner of the world where they can be worthwhile and happy. I feel for them, we support each other, have lived through so much together, and look forward to the future, though often not physically together, but spiritually. Can't wait to see Cath. This afternoon I'll go to Tufts to see Liu Mei-chun and call Professors. Off we go. I hope a decision comes a little close this week.

July 21, 1983

Sitting at Cathy's desk here in her room at Tufts. I almost feel as if she's here with me, although I know she's far away in Costa Rica.

It's so good to see Liu Mei-chun again. As I was writing to Cath last night, it's as if there was a connection between Liu Mei-chun's and my thoughts this past year. There is a deep understanding between us. Liu Mei-chun and her husband are special people. Like many Chinese, they are cheerful and have time to talk.

Confusing times. I guess I was foolish enough to think I would find answers here to grad school and profession questions. Of course, I have not. The answers are within me, perhaps. I have a few more appointments this week; perhaps something concrete will come of those, perhaps not. There are still a few people back in Chicago that I'll talk to and then I'll try and make a commitment of some kind. Third World Development. Business school or PhD.

I don't know why I felt so let down talking to Professor Klein. I guess I needed a pep talk. Someone to go on and on about a bright future. But he was too busy talking about these "other" brilliant people he knew. I need someone to say, "With your particular talents perhaps you should. . ." But I guess no one wants to stand out on a limb like that. I understand.

The campus looks beautiful. Déjà vu, that's for sure.

The phone call to China was wonderful. Although Ruo-xin wasn't there, his brother was. What a treat. I want to go back so badly. Perhaps if I had a plan here that really turned me on I wouldn't feel that way. But as of today, I feel like spending the rest of my days in China. Is there anything for me here?

Events, events. All I write about is what, where, when, and how it was. But this time has included another dimension. Perhaps the greatest crossroads I have come upon so far, is now. Or this period of time. Not that anything is permanent or any decision is final. But I think about things these days unlike I ever thought before I went to China. Being with Liu Mei-chun and her husband these past few days has brought the ideas to the surface.

How's this for a scenario: China. She lives there for two years. Comes home. Goes to grad school two years. Leaves it all. Returns to China. Forever comes and goes.

Liu Mei-chun is going through a lot now. She's about to leave here, after such an amazing experience. So, she is evaluating. The good and the bad here and in China. I see my own society for all its honor and preciousness and evil so much more clearly now that I have seen another. And so does Liu Mei-chun.

July 22, 1983

Back at Tufts I knew a woman, Zhou Tsai Qin. Not only did she direct some of the most challenging and successful theatre that I have ever performed, but she also was my first taste of China. As I made my way into the hours of her days and nights, I learned of her philosophy of life, her strength and spirit. Watching her father Zhou Xin Fang (the famous child star of Shanghai's opera), slaughtered at the hands of the Red Guard during the Cultural Revolution did not crush Tsai. She has gone on to teach, to nurture, to spread the word of the importance of discipline and honesty in theatre and in life. I owe so much to her.

Finally, I got to see her. Elated. I never thought I would get the chance to see her again. It was almost unreal. After all these years of thinking about her.

Tsai explained my history to the people at the dinner party. They couldn't believe it—an actress (Tsai will always remember me that way) who was an international relations major, going back to China to take economics and history. I am made up of so many facets. I guess I have already led so many lives in these twenty-two years.

Zhou Tsai Qin has aged only physically. Her spirit, vitality, and energy are still as vital as ever. And finally to talk with her in Chinese. So much time has come and gone. We talked—I mostly listened to their discussion—about art and theatre in China and here in the States. Listened to them go on and on about why Zhou Xin Fang was such an amazing actor. The four Chinese in that living room were so different than most Chinese I know. First, because they are artists and second, because they have a strong affinity with the Western world. It's not just the blue jeans, but also the informal attitude. It was interesting to chat with them.

"How do you feel differently than before you left for China?" one of Tsai's guests asked me. I answered that I have become more accepting of people, and I appreciate so much more the luxury, the freedom in which I live. I realize, too, how hard Americans work for what they want. Second, on the more depressing side, I realize how screwy American relationships can be. Lousy, compared to the relationships that take place, the mutual support and friendships I have found with the Chinese. I find social relationships with my Chinese friends so much more satisfying than with most Americans, with the exception of my closest friends and family.

Talked with Tony for hours before and after we dropped them off at Houston Hall at Tufts. Good old Houston Hall. Tony. He is really intense. Humorous and serious. So wrapped up in analyzing his and others' feelings. Americans are a strange breed. I love it. They really like to delve deep into thoughts and emotions, sit at the bar and talk for hours. And so many kinds of folks—all shapes and sizes, all different schools of thoughts, dress, style, on and on—bound by an aching desire to communicate, to give and share and be loved. Not that I identify across the board, either. No. But I love to be with them, too. Being close to some of them is good, interesting, and rewarding.

Professor Quinn says: Make up your own mind. Take some responsibility and make a decision about what you want to do.

Oh, so easy to give such advice. So hard to do.

Relax for today. Think on it awhile.

Must write Ruo-xin.

August 6, 1983

Thirty-four year anniversary of Hiroshima. And the world has never been the same. Never the same.

The new system of international relationships that has evolved is full of potential and problems. Perhaps with degrees in economic development and business I can put my two cents into the process. It's a fascinating field and a place where we need people of practicality, broad perspective, empathy, creativity, and skill.

So, yes, I've decided what I want to go to grad school in. Whether I'll have the money to do it is another question. Christ, I hate how money tries to rule our lives. But for today, my thoughts are not on that subject. In nine days I'll be on my way to China. Back to China, to explore for eight short months, back to the love of my life. I got a tape from him today. It was clear that tape talks are a new experience for him, but he did quite well for a beginner. A bit too much talk about the weather, but heat can be overwhelming. He told me about the class trip, climbing the mountains, collecting birds and animals and snakes. Watching the sun rise. It was an eye-opener for him to see some new areas of China, the smaller towns.

Joint military maneuvers between the U.S. and Honduras began today. God help us. I do not support our actions in Central America and I never have. I do not support the spread of U.S. arms material around the world. We are going to be responsible for our own destruction.

Cathy comes home in six days. I can't wait to see her. Her picture sits on my desk. I'm ready for the real thing.

As I lay on the couch last night nursing my sore jaw (having just had all four wisdom teeth taken out), who should drop in but my high school classmate and soulmate, James. Hammerman. Now that was a treat. Working for a world of understanding, and change in our society through nonviolent methods, he has an alive, creative mind. We sat on the couch and chatted about it all with Mom and Dad. Later on, they bought us ice cream and we sat and ate it and talked about the path: which to choose, how to go—for Jim at this point in his life. I'll always treasure our friendship.

This summer I've been reading *Red Star Over China*. The beginning: the basis, ideals, seeds of the movement. It began as such a fine thing. I would have joined, too, had I been a Chinese at that time. And what a special breed of people they were.

But the times changed. The movement lost the purity that it almost really never had. So much of it I believe in. But I have such a hard time with a concept that does not come naturally to people, that has to be taught. Forced. Their brains have to be educated, brainwaves rerouted from selfishness to mutual support. From "Me is the number one survival instinct" to "Me no longer." Rather, the "group" is the new "Me" that counts.

Sweet man, will our lives together ever really happen? Is it really what you want? Will you endure a year of separation?

Daddy seems buried in his financial pressures sometimes. So complicated.

Every day now, I feel as if I'm waiting to return. Not only to return to China, but to him. To Beijing. To a land that has caught me in her web in every way. A fascination. A curiosity. A feeling of being at home and at the same time so far away. Isolated and yet so intricately involved. And in love with a man there. So in love with him that I can't wait a second more to see him again. And yet, I could wait for years. He's there. Alive. Our communication goes on even twelve thousand miles apart. A soul I cannot live without. It's almost a scary thing to realize. And maybe not even true. But he has, he has changed my life. I am waiting now, simply waiting to be with him again.

There's no place like home. And I am happy here. But I won't feel right until I'm with him again. I'll miss home the minute I set foot on China's soil. But I look past those tears to see his face waiting there for me. And that's all that counts for now.

August 12, 1983

Why can't I sleep? My sweetheart, I miss you.

But tomorrow I have to get up early. I have things to get done, etc. I can't not have slept the night before.

I'm worried about school, where to find the best economic development program, what to do with it. Worries—there always are a few. After such a wonderful evening with the family, celebrating Peter's birthday, why can't I just forget about the daily worries and rest for a while?

I must be going to China.

Part III

重返中國

Return to China
1983

August 22, 1983
  At Shi Fan University

Fade out.

Fade in.

It's like a dream, a movie, a novel, whatever you like. I'm back. And it is so good to be here. The trip up from Hong Kong, I must admit, was not my favorite—to say the least. Mostly because I had to drag around so much baggage.

But in a flash, I woke up to the sound of train tracks rushing underneath me, clickety-clack, as the sun rose over the Chinese countryside. A bit different feeling than the first time I made that trek from Hong Kong up to Beijing. First, because I could communicate with the people around me. Second, because I knew what to expect at the end of the line. Third, Ruo-xin. Sweet man. Now, more than ever, I can't believe he's for real.

Till later. Have to go find a key and a light bulb for this room. It's a grey, rainy day; light bulbs are certainly in order.

August 23, 1983

Spent the day, what a way to spend the day. I could make this a habit, that's for sure. Up at six o'clock (I'm still too jumpy to sleep much later that that), breakfast at seven. Ruo-xin came over at half past eight before he went to the classroom to study. I don't know what came over me yesterday; I was just so afraid that some professor would come knocking on the door and that would be the end of us. He was good about it, of course, and cheered me up. We spent a nice afternoon at Bei Hai park talking and listening to music, watching the people.

Anyway, I felt more relaxed this morning. It takes a while to get adjusted. Sat and wrote a letter to Mom and Dad and the clan, turned out to be fourteen pages long; I had a lot to say. And I know they're curious about how Ruo-xin is handling everything. He's fabulous. Not perfect (he's not as awake as I am in the morning), but he's something else. I never thought I'd meet anyone good enough. I know. That's a pompous thing to say. But you must admit my attitude toward everyday living is a special one. I never thought—and I never found anyone who shared that attitude, my temperament, until I met himself.

Then, off to the dentist to see about my infected gum. No problem. Penicillin and an herbel mouthwash will do the trick. Lunch and then a nice nap. Heaven on earth. Woke up at about one o'clock and made the English practice tape for Ruo-xin. We spoke English at the park yesterday. He did far better than I had expected. Smart boy. Then I wrote to Berkeley and added a note to Mom and Dad. And here I am, it's four o'clock and himself will be here soon.

Talking to Ruo-xin's friend last night reminded me how different street talk is from the language I speak with most people here. So much to learn.

Make-up on the faces of the girls here. Flip me out. Things are changing fast.

August 24, 1983

The doubts are emerging. Although we have decided that education should be in the States, the rest is up in the air: to live here or there. As Ruo-xin said, and his sister said, we'll simply have to see how we feel after we've both graduated.

As we rode on the bus yesterday, I pictured us ten years from now, coming back to China to visit his family. How will he feel then as he sits on the bus watching his countrymen ride by on their bicycles? He will wonder what his life would have been like had he not left this world behind. As the airplane lands back in the U.S., I imagine I will breathe a sigh of relief to be home again. But will he? Will the States ever feel like home to him? Probably not. At the same time, now, both Ruo-xin and his sister have said that they're afraid I wouldn't be able to really adjust to a lifetime here in China. Who can say?

We talked about work and how family will always be the priority. I tried to explain my feelings about work, my sense of responsibility toward the U.S. relationship with the Third World. My peers, a few anyway, can understand and empathize with that feeling. But he is a *part* of the Third World; he couldn't possibly empathize with how I feel, not right now anyway.

There's another reason, I've discovered, why I want to marry Ruo-xin. He appreciates. First, he appreciates me. For my confidence, my ability, attitude, ableness. He's not threatened by it. And he appreciates the strengths in others, as well as in himself. I have a hand up, and it's based only on experience. I've never truly been appreciated by the men I've loved. And I find so many men caught up in their own egos that they are oblivious to the talents of people around them—particularly those of women. I realize, however, that this is only one kind of man. There are others, who do appreciate their wives for their talents. Daddy does, to a certain extent. As does Peter. I'm not sure about Joey because I've never come to know a relationship of his closely enough.

In my family's world, I was brought up to be so conscious of the have-nots in the world. And my generation really saw the Third World on the rise in its importance to the rest of the world. I've seen the world as my home for so many years now. I've gone through all kinds of relationships, most of them positive, but certainly topsy turvy and never really fulfilling. My demands were for a truly liberated man who loved life as much as I did and loved me even more. I was always searching for some new color, a change from my peaceful, if not somewhat boring suburban life. It's so obvious why I've chosen this road, if you look at my history and what makes up my hopes and desires and needs. And that's why we marry, anyway, isn't it? To fulfill our needs by fulfilling those of someone else? That's part of it.

This disturbing, and perhaps, too one-sided, book called the *Broken Earth* has made me wonder all over again how the Chinese really feel about their situation today. How they see the revolution, the good changes; what were they? And the bad changes; what were they? How do they really feel about communism, if they feel about it at all? Who among them believes China will really be able to modernize? Who does not believe? Who has given up hope? Why? Why not? And other questions that I'm sure another cup of coffee and some more thought will stir up. Now I can speak their language and understand it. Now is the time to ask these questions—and not just of university students, but of peasants and workers, too. Only eight months left. Better start soon.

August 26, 1983

Chinese version of a car wash: everyone gathers around the water pipe that is sticking out of the ground. A hose is attached to the pipe. One student kneels down to take charge of the hose while the others bring their bicycles up, one by one, to receive a wash-down. Everyone watches attentively, conversation is as lively as the spray of water coming out of the hose. A sweet scene.

August 27, 1983

An evening to remember.

Ruo-xin, his brother Ruo-ji, sister Ruo-yi, and her husband. After a meal together that was particulary lively, we all trooped off to Tian An Men Square on this summer night. Strolled through the Forbidden City, out onto Chang An Avenue, and over to the square. Just as we walked up to the border of the square, Ruo-ji recalled the 1976 demonstration after the death of Zhou En Lai.

"It was an ocean of people." The days when the square was a place for demonstration. He was there.

We walked into the center and sat down. In a tight circle we sat, cross-legged. Chatted. The past. The present. The future. This was the first we had mentioned to the family that I would only be staying one more year here in China. Ruo-ji was surprised, but seemed to take it quite well.

His sister: such a sweet woman. Thirty-eight now. Very thoughtful—perhaps too much. Like me, her nerves give her stomach a hard time. Sweet, shining smile. She does love her brothers, as if there were no one else. However, she married a man equally wonderful and equally entertaining. Talkative and vivacious.

"But blue eyes..." he said while were sitting in the square, "blue eyes are scary. I can't adjust to the blue eyes of foreigners. Black eyes are best."

"It seems like they wouldn't be able to see with blue eyes. With black eyes I feel like we can see much more clearly," Ruo-xin said, laughing at the silliness of a comment he still sort of believed. Scientific or not, there are certain perceptions, ideas, that are hard to change.

How I can take him away from this wonderful family, I just don't know. I come home from their house at night with such a warm feeling. The strength of family, of siblings enjoying one another's company. A nice feeling to go to sleep with.

August 28, 1983   *Sunday*

Just before a storm. Gray skies, winds through the trees rustle the leaves outside my window. Loud claps of thunder. Strings of lightning.

Flute music on the radio.

The dorm is quiet.

I'm back in China. Back in China. Back in Beijing.

Freeze the time.

Later on: Note—the beginning of a list of ways Ruo-xin was affected by Mao.

Number One, Mao felt strongly about self-criticism, the importance of cleaning out, purifying, continually rectifying the innermost self. With all sincerity, Ruo-xin has told me many a time to tell him of his weak points, whenever I might happen to see or think of one.

Number Two, Mao's feelings about learning and being unbalanced: too much head and no soul. Although later on in his career Mao certainly became fanatical about this concept, there is something to be gleaned from it. So, on the one hand, Ruo-xin is as hard a worker as I am and loves to learn—when it's of interest to him. But at the same time, he's itching to get out and work. More often than not, when the question of how to work things out in the U.S. comes up, Ruo-xin talks about the importance of working part time when he's going to school in the U.S. It's true, he doesn't really know what that means and how work will infringe upon his time. But perhaps that's only my spoiled point of view.

August 30, 1983

My first day of classes.

I have only one comment for now and it sums up how I feel for the most part: If only I could find Professor Hannigan right now, I would tell him how fabulous he is, and how amazingly open and progressive his American History class was. God help these people here. Their minds will never know.

September 3, 1983

Sitting in my sunny room on this Saturday afternoon, learning a few new Cheng yu (Chinese idiomatic phrases), when I looked out my window and what did I see? A team of twenty professors out under the hot sun doing manual labor. Cutting grass by hand. Ding and Shu, An and Blinky, and some others who I didn't recognize. Shu was in his shorts and T-shirt like most of the men. They all looked quite comfortable and fit quite naturally into the setting, despite the hot temps, the dust, and having to bend over for an hour or so pulling grass.

Were they recalling the years of labor during the Cultural Revolution?

I felt spoiled and soft and too sheltered.

I guess it's a little like church. Labor and cleanse your soul of any possible dirt—dirt such as thoughts of intellectuals being better or more valuable than peasants. Look, we can read *and* cut grass.

One day, if we do this enough, the whole world will be one class and...classless.

Dream on....

But, as Marx said, whatever turns you on! Marx???!

September 16, 1983

A month ago I was standing in O'Hare Airport saying goodbye to Mom and Dad and Cath. Wanting to stay, itching to go. Now, I'm sitting in a full classroom in the history building. All around me sit my Chinese classmates; 95 percent of them are practicing English out loud. It's still a funny feeling for me: to be surrounded by all these people practicing my language. But then again, I've devoted a major portion of my time in the past four years to learning their language. I should be able to empathize. But so many of them, all learning English. To top it off, the French and the Japanese in the dormitory know English, too. Blow me away. "How do I distinguish between *th* and *s*?" the student next to me asks. "How do you pronounce these sounds?"

Joanne arrived yesterday.

Bubbling and excited. Chinese-American. The usual story, she related to me in a whispered voice. Her parents fled the revolution in '48. Went to Taiwan. Finally moved to the States.

10:10 Ugh....exhausted.

September 19, 1983

And I was so healthy! Up until Saturday, when I got a cold, which yesterday turned into exactly what I got last year when I first arrived: the cough, unable to breathe, my lungs totally out to lunch. I could feel it coming on the night our friends from Hangzhou came for dinner. All I wanted to do was get out of that tiny room and sit outside where Mrs. Li always sits. Just to breathe. I'll never forget it—feeling so sad, and not knowing why. Ruo-xin so concerned. He decided that a walk was what I needed. As we rounded the corner to head back to the house, Ruo-ji came walking down the lane with two chairs in his hand.

"Sit here and chat for a while." He knows us too well, I guess. Or we're easy to read. So, in the grey alley we sat on the chairs, enjoying the cool night air. I felt better. Ruo-ji came back a few minutes later with a plate of melon for us to eat. Ruo-xin's sister, Jie Jie, came and joined us, too. Ah, to be able to freeze the time.

Mom and Dad's tape responding to my thoughts on freedom was too great. As much as they claim how my thoughts on the subject really set them to thinking, so it is the same effect of their thoughts on me. It's true, I never really thought of it that way. Freedom is a responsibility. Because just as we have the freedom to take action, voice our opinions, and try to make changes, so does it give us the choice to do nothing, to become a victim of government, welfare, and other evils. Once we have freedom, it is our responsibility to make sure we use it for the good of the people, always to be sure that our freedoms are kept intact and forever upheld. It is not an easy task.

As I sit here in bed recuperating, Ruo-xin sits at my desk studying something or other about the human chemistry whatever. Chemistry. If only I had another life, I would explore the world of human chemistry and biology. Why? Because probably the basis of my struggle is to understand what really makes me and others around me tick. Is it chemicals and brain waves and nerve impulses that really make us feel what we feel, react how we react—is it pure science that makes up our souls? Or is there something more spiritual than that? I tend to believe there isn't, but then why do I cry at the first snowfall? Why does my love feel so. . . so spiritual, nonmaterial, so beyond this earth? Finally, I hit a question where I discover that a "happy medium" answer is not sufficient, not at all satisfactory. How can the way I react to—for example, a good lecture, getting all worked up—be simply a spiritual nonphysical reaction? But then—is it perhaps first an input of idea-thoughts, which stimulates brain waves, which gets the adrenaline running, which makes a physical reaction—which makes us feel the feeling we call "excited" or "moved" or whatever?

But to be able to spend a lifetime studying science, to get an idea of what is or isn't at the base of our emotions—that would be fulfilling. I think all this started when I realized how every month, just a day or two before my period, I feel like crying—all day long. Right before the hormones are about to crash, I feel totally frazzled. Or when I drink coffee, I am easily brought to tears.

What about when I listen to music: how that can raise an array of different emotions, which usually take on a physical character of laughter, tears, a rise in blood pressure. Is sadness an emotion or a chemical reaction to stimuli? Or is emotion chemical? Or does emotion send off a physical reaction, which then gives the emotion a physical character?

Anyway, Ruo-xin has been taking such sweet care of me, particularly since I got sick. Buying me my meals, bringing them over here, and feeding me. Always refilling the mug with water to ensure that I drink enough fluids. And today, running all over to find a doctor, carrying me through the crazy inefficient maze created by socialist medical care. Ugh! Talk about sloppy! The emergency department was a building that even a detective would have a hard time finding. And once we got there, as I lay on the bench suffocating, he ran around trying to find a doctor who was supposed to be "just down the hall." Right! Just down the hall, my ass. More like out to lunch. And once he started examining me, he took fifteen minutes just to write everything out—while I lay there feeling like I was going to die. I let Ruo-xin go get the medicine as soon as the doctor prescribed it, because I know what a major hassle that always is.

Now, however, I feel a lot better. If only the screwy doctor's salary depended upon his performance, today would have been a hell of a lot easier. But Ruo-xin put up with it quite well.

September 20, 1983

And why not? He's used to it.

Peter Drew Carlson's birthday was yesterday.

Protests against Marcos and calls for his resignation in the wake of the murder of his opponent before elections, which are to take place later this year. U.S. Navy ships firing against Druse forces in the mountains of Lebanon. The Soviet Union and United States continue to squabble over the South Korean jet airliner dispute. Arms talks continue.

September 22, 1983   *The day before autumn officially begins on*

My favorite season is about to begin.

So strange. While reading the *Economic Daily* on problems about supply of stove pipes, of all things, Bruce Chang comes slipping into my thoughts. Pictures in my mind of the red room, the closet next to his bed, the smell of incense. The tiny bathroom, cluttered. Early mornings, taking taxis back to Tufts from Cambridge. Crazy days.

Why should they pop into my head now? Is he over on the other side of the world thinking about me? Or is he in trouble? Or perhaps he just died a few moments ago.

And here I sit in China, loving my man and reading about prospects for stove pipe shortages this winter.

September 25, 1983

Just when I thought I was getting better—shit. Got a nice, juicy cold. Can't do a thing. Totally unproductive. Ugh. But sweet Ruo-xin is taking such good care of me. How did I live so many years without his friendship? I wonder.

I am just now beginning to see clearly the real differences of how and what Americans think versus Chinese. Since I've been sick this past week, I've been going to the foreign students' cafeteria for meals. There I had a chance to converse with my American classmates. Like today, for example, we spent a few hours talking about love and religion and ideas we base our lives on. That's not to say that the Chinese don't talk about these things—they do—but very seldom, and only in private. They'd be more apt to talk about the job allocation question than about love and religion, as Ruo-xin pointed out.

Laura summed it up quite well when she said the Americans have the luxury and leisure time to think in the abstract. Chinese perhaps do not. Moreover, Americans feel that discussing issues from government to world problems to social issues is worthwhile, that perhaps their feelings make a difference, that it is almost, as some people feel, a responsibility to go over these issues. Whereas most Chinese feel it makes little difference discussing such issues. Their opinions lie far from the decision-making process of government, which covers education, ethics, day/living from life earth.

And here I stand, in the middle of two worlds. What's even stranger is how Ruo-xin's thoughts have been influenced by my world and have begun to enjoy searching through the world of other issues, and how I, on the other hand, have gotten used to days on end without a political or "other worldly" discussion.

When I look into the eyes of some of my American classmates, I recall another life I had years ago. For a moment I naively believe that these people—or these kinds of people—can send me back to that world. But as Joanne pointed out, you can never go back to life as an undergraduate. Sure, I'll go back to America, but life will never be as it was before, and for the most part, though not entirely, nor would I want it back.

It seems like such a long time since this morning when Ruo-xin came by to boil the pear drink for my cough.

September 26, 1983

OK. I gave in for a week. Didn't go to class, rested, allowed my body to dictate the plan of the day (with the exception of writing grad school applications). But enough is enough. A week is long enough. Now I'm in charge and the old body had better just hang on for the ride and not put up a fuss. I don't have any more spare time for illness.

Today was probably the most productive day all week. Got through a good portion of economics this afternoon. My friend, Number One Dragon, came by this evening to chat. Stayed for a few hours. Talked about last year. He has such an innocent way of looking at things.

"Sometimes Tom—I mean, one day, I came in the room and he didn't greet me happily like he usually did. What was wrong?" One incident still loomed so huge in his memory.

As it turns out (much to Joanne's disappointment), he wants to read the Bible for the literary purpose. Reading Milton and other Western writers, he finds it difficult to understand the real meaning of the essays without understanding the Biblical parallels.

Met Ruo-xin at the classroom at nine o'clock. We hopped on a bicycle and rode around the back paths, grapevines, and shacks behind the school. There was a strong wind and the leaves whispered to us as we rode along. Dust whipped up around us on the road. We chatted about the day, about the GMAT, and whether or not I should go to Hong Kong. It was a sweet ride. . . . sweet smiles.

September 28, 1983

Spent the morning in the periodicals room. Because there are no copy machines available, to get a copy of an article I have to copy the whole thing by hand. I've been working on an article for four sittings now. I know, problems will come with the modernization of China—but at least they'll have copy machines.

October 4, 1983   *6:00 pm*

When the sun sets, it always feels like such an emotional time. You'd think a human being would get used to the setting of the sun since it happens every night. Sometime I feel joyous, sometimes sad.

I'm here, building may own life, I should feel free and happy. And with the man I love (except he's so often in class), studying, experimenting, learning, living, loving.

But the pressures are sometimes too much. I feel sad, far away from home and alone.

October 5, 1983

Wrote Mom instead of writing in this journal.

October 8, 1983

Sure, you might think this Saturday would pass just like all other Saturdays here in Beijing. But this is a special day. After weeks of searching and trying to convince Ruo-xin's father that the Li family shouldn't pay for the ring, we are going to buy it—at the Beijing Hotel. We have our one-year engagement anniversary this month. The first year of many. And it was a wonderful year.

I sit here and find it a little difficult to believe that this is really happening to me, the girl who planned on staying single forever. Through the most depressing of my days, he can come and pick me up like no one else I know. Such a fine spirit and a thoughtful soul. Really, I sit here and find it hard to believe that I really found him.

It's a blue-skied fall day.

Typed applications in the morning as I sat in Grandma's robe and my long underwear. Drank coffee. Listened to Dan Fogelberg. Went to lunch and sat with my buddies from the biology department. Wu Xiao Ping, Li Hua, the class monitor's girlfriend, and a few others. Chit-chat. Cheerful. Pleasant.

A few nights ago Wu Xiao Ping and I sat in her dorm room and talked about the sensitive subject of male-female relationships and what the Chinese call "looking for a friend." She just hasn't found anyone suitable here at school, except one, and he's a resident of Beijing and she's not so that's out. But there's a common Chinese fear that if a girl graduates from college without a boyfriend, she will have a hard time finding one once she starts work.

"And I'm so tall," she said to me seriously. "There aren't too many tall boys, you know."

Before I became serious about Ruo-xin, I had always thought the two of them would make a cute couple.

Sitting at lunch she told me how antsy and mischievous Ruo-xin was during labor time today. "He threw a stone at me," she said. And then he finally just left. Unable to concentrate on labor that morning, I have no doubt.

As we sat last night and talked about his frustration about being pampered by his family, and about his fear of my feeling neglected when he focuses more on the Li family at times, I thought back to the earlier days last year and how much he's grown since then. Like my brother Peter, once he found the right girl, he turned into a man and a mensch.

Two nights ago, my fears about grad school finally came to the surface. Fears about will I ever be content with my job if I'm not accepted to grad school, fears about supporting our family, on and on.

"You can only do your best," he reminded me. "After that, one must accept the results and learn to make the best of the new conditions."

"We'll do it," he said, holding me tight. "We have spirit, two strong spirits. You must not be afraid." He asked concrete questions about which part of the applications I was unsure about and where could he help me. But he really can't help me with this; he can only support me.

"I could get help from Nathan or my father if I were in the U.S.," I blurted out.

Silence.

"Sometimes I feel as if you'd do better if I weren't in your life," he said. No sooner had he said those words than he regretted saying them. I told him never to repeat such a thing again and that I didn't hear it this time. I was flabbergasted. But, yes, I know many others have wondered the same question about our relationship. All that matters to me is I know they're wrong—and now Ruo-xin does, too. He's the best thing that has ever or will ever happen in my life. I couldn't have even dreamed of someone more fitting. And we are an unbeatable team. Like bamboo that bends in the wind but does not break. With the bamboo theory and our strong love, there's no stopping us. Happiness is ours; struggle is, too. And we're ready.

This afternoon, my finger receives her new life long partner. My heart was bound to him as long ago as last winter, as was his to mine. But now, as a part of custom, we seal the bond with an object. And so it goes.

What a gorgeous day.

October 9, 1983

Will you ever forget it? Never. We both took deep breaths as we walked up to the counter. The first really big item we've invested in together. And now everything is official.

Back at home, we sat in the living room with his mother. I had her put it on first because in reality she would have still been wearing hers, if she hadn't had to sell it when they were starving in the sixties.

I looked at the new ring on her old finger and felt a sense of hope, of continuation.

He actually put it on my finger twice.

The first time was just when Mama was there. He sat on the big chair and I sat next to Mama. He took my hand and put it on.

In English, he said, "I love you forever."

"And I love you forever." Two kisses on the cheeks, and there it was.

As he said later on the bus going home, the ring is simply an expression of our love. But the depth of our love is priceless, far beyond the price of the ring. Well said, my man.

Then, when the whole family was there sitting at the table, Ruo-ji burst into smiles. "Come on! Let's see it!" And with everyone there, sitting all together around the little table, he put it on my finger again. (I had put it back in the box.) We repeated our little ceremony and everyone was glowing. We toasted to happiness and a fruitful life—and to grow old together, please. And that was it.

Sweet time.

This morning at breakfast, a whole bunch of us sat at the table and enjoyed the high spirits. Talked about Chinese courtship practices and on and on. Eating our sweetened rice gruel, we all couldn't have been happier. Glowing faces.

After all is said and done, I think of the lonely times, the happy times—it all works out. Sure, I thought of Peter Drew yesterday, my first love. And Brian, and Nathan. Sweet, sure, but bitter at the same time, those days. That world is gone, and a new world has begun.

Got to write applications for Fletcher and Harvard today. Get to it.

October 17, 1983

Last night I surprised my in-laws by arriving after dinner. At half past five I woke up and my stomach was better. So I got up, leaped on the bus, and headed for Den Shi Kou street.

"Hey! Look who's here!"

"I feel better, Ba Ba. So I came."

Ruo-xin appeared in the doorway, a broad smile across his face. "Wonderful!"

"I missed you too much," I said, as I put my arm around his neck and hugged him, laughing. Ruo-xin blushed and everyone laughed at our open display of affection.

It had been a gorgeous day. Moving the furniture in my room, cleaning the place up.

"One day, we'll be fixing up our own home," I said. One day... But now I wonder, where? Will it be here or back in the U.S.?

Both of us exhausted, we fell asleep on the couch-bed with the sun shining on us. Woke up half an hour later and went to the cafeteria for lunch.

I went to the Free Market that afternoon. What a zoo! I ran into some especially sweet smiles, bought some pears and a few paintings.

That evening before dinner, we looked through an old scrapbook. Pictures Ruo-xin had painted, quotes Ruo-ji had collected during middle school, and notes from Ruo-ji's classmates, written in the early sixties. "Upon your graduation, I hope you continue to work for the mother country and continue the struggle towards communism."

The year 1976. Every month a major incident took place here in China. Ruo-xin told me about the day Mao died. It happened that they were shopping that afternoon. At half past three, the news announced that at four o'clock there would be an important news report. Everyone should stop to listen.

At four o'clock, the news was announced that Mao had died. People made their way home, Ruo-xin told me, some crying as they rode through the streets.

"Did you cry?"

"No. . . . But I was very sad. Scared without Mao Ze Dong. What will China do?"

Later during dinner, we saw a news clip about the UN supply of grain problem. Got on the subject of the U.S. government's latest agricultural program, PIK.

Jie Jie piped in, "Of course, it's just the big capitalists who wanted such a program."

"No!" I said angrily.

"There are good capitalists and bad capitalists. Some capitalists are not exploiters of the workers. Some are. Some work for the good of other people. This plan was made by capitalists just like the rest of the capitalists in the U.S. But the only difference is, this is a government plan, made out of fear of the rebellion of an unhappy farming populace. It's not simply because they are capitalists. We all are capitalists for the most part. It's because they are selfish government, selfish planners."

Jie Jie was a little surprised by my outburst. But she did learn something.

Last night was a night for political issues. The executions in Tibet were subject of the conversation, courtesy of me.

"Of course," Ruo-ji said, "they were political dissidents. That's why they were executed. Perhaps they were working for the independence of Tibet. Our government fears that."

I'm afraid this government crack-down that has begun is more than just for the safety of the streets. It coincides exactly with the cleaning out of the Communist Party's bad elements. Some of it is necessary. There's a lot of corruption. But anyone who doesn't agree with Deng's policies is out. Even the *People's Daily* said yesterday we have to be careful not to get carried away and let this turn into another Cultural Revolution.

With the economic system loosening up and material life getting better every day, a tightening of social controls seems to be the planned method to keep away the ugly capitalist notions that can come with material desires and wealth. This they call the anti-spiritual pollution movement. It is a movement designed to clamp down on and stamp out Western influence.

I hope it doesn't get to out of hand—if it hasn't already.

October 18, 1983

I protest. Why am I always the first one to say "I love you?" Even when I see it written all over his face, shining in his eyes, I still am the first to say it.

Silly girl. Instead of saying so in words, he expresses it in actions. I get off the bus today and whose face meets mine? Ruo-xin's. Aglow. Huge smile out of sight. Surprises in seeing one another so unexpectedly. Where had he been? He'd been running around the city trying to find an electric hot plate for me.

And if I hadn't run into him just then and asked him where he had been, he'd never have told me that he had spent all that time running around, using up precious study time, to find me a hot plate.

Sweet love. It's true, you don't need to say so first. I can see it in your eyes, feel it in your heart, and see it in your actions and how you live every day.

October 21, 1983   *Friday morning*

I don't know why I thought of it this morning. I guess it's because it's come up so often lately.

Chinese people saying goodbye to other Chinese—for example, family members. Jie Fu leaving with his wife to go to Anhui. There he was, saying goodbye to Ruo-xin and his brother. No hug. Not even shaking hands. Just smiles and words like "study hard" and "take care of yourself." Where were the hugs? Where were the "I love you"s? I've seen quite a few goodbyes in quite a few families—and never did they hug or kiss. Or when saying hello after a long time apart. In public, never a kiss hello or a hug. It's very Chinese, if you'll excuse the expression.

Ruo-xin and I were discussing the issue. "You realize," he said to me, "the feelings are the same. We just express them differently."

True. True. That cannot be disputed. It's funny, Wednesday when I sat talking with Jie Jie, she and I hugged and pressed cheeks as we laughed about something, I forget what. Mao Gao. Her little boy, who was standing in front of us said, "They're kissing."

The whole family laughed. She and Ruo-xin are actually inclined to express what they feel—at least more so than other Chinese I've known, besides Liu Mei-chun and her husband. Thank goodness. But I really never have been able to build a relationship if at some point some emotion wasn't expressed. Even in the first five months when we were "just friends," eyes sparkled. No hands touched. But the eyes...

After a while, it naturally occurs; eyes aren't enough. And slowly, month after month, new expressions appear. Still, last night was the first time Ruo-xin said "I love you" before I said it. That was really something.

OK. Let's get this show on the road. Today it's Michigan's essay. Ugh.

October 25, 1983

Today, Ruo-xin and I officially celebrate our one-year anniversary of meeting each other. Two people who have found something so precious together.

But look. Look at the world that surrounds them.

Sunday, the senseless bombing in Beirut where over one hundred American marines were killed.

Two major reports on the greenhouse effect just came out. Because of our earlier failure to develop another source of fuel beyond fossil fuels, there is a buildup of CO_2 thus,we human beings in our efforts to survive are slowly laying grounds for our own destruction.

The arms talks in a deadlock. Missiles aimed and ready if one day all else fails.

The picture is two people, a young man and a young woman, one Chinese, one Caucasian, clinging to one another as the black clouds gather. They promise their love forever, for 80 years they say, wondering what 80 years will feel like and if they really can live to be 102 years old together. Hoping.

But as the storm clouds of pollution, war, and revolution draw in, even their love, so strong, so spirited, will be suffocated before it's time.

Nice thought for the morning, Spero.

Sometimes I feel as if we've been cursed with a world we didn't even build. We want our children to see life. Because of the mistakes of our forefathers, what world will there be left for our offspring?

Write your applications and don't give up. Even if the world can't be saved, you've got to try. Remember our motto.

October 27, 1983

The past few days have seemed like an eon.

Papa Sal is dead, and it has left me with a sad, empty feeling. One more connection with the Grandma Bess I never knew is gone. Whenever I was with Papa Sal, he was so warm and loving. Such a papa. Everytime I was with him I felt as if Grandma Bess were somewhere not far away. I didn't realize he was eighty years old. I wonder how Speedy must feel. After so many years together, it's just not fair to be separated.

People in our extended family are slowly but surely passing away, and I'm afraid. Afraid that we, the next generation, somehow won't be able to cultivate the kind of united family atmosphere that our older generation has cultivated for us. I know that's nonsense. And why ask for a repeat? But I can't help but remember, picture it so clearly in my mind, feel it in my bones, sitting in the Shattens' living room on a snowy winter day when I was twelve, playing monopoly or watching TV. Everyone was there.

And then one by one, they're gone. It's only slowly that I have come to realize the mortality of myself and those close to me.

It's strange then maybe not so strange. After I got the letter from Daddy and felt the immediate wish of sadness, I began to feel strangely angry. It doesn't make any sense. Why angry? Maybe it was because the thought of not being there to tell Papa Sal how much he meant to me, just once more.

Or maybe—I know I felt the feelings all over again of wishing till it hurt that I had known Grandma Bess. What would her influence on my life have been had she lived? And what would it have meant for Daddy and Mom still to share nice times with her?

China is so far away from home sometimes. Anger doesn't make any sense—but it's what I felt. And then finally that night, simply vacant. I sat up in bed and read Simone de Beauvoir for a few hours until Ruo-xin came. I could only look at him with blank eyes. I didn't feel like anything. Just empty. We chatted for a while, but I felt as if I were not there.

The note about my *magna cum laude* from Tufts went almost unfelt. Even though I worked so hard all those years, I didn't think much of it yesterday.

Today was better in that I felt more alive, but no less angry. All it took to set me off again was to hear over the Voice of America that the U.S. sent troops into invade Grenada.

What a bastard he is, that Reagan. Won't anyone ever put a stop to our path of foreign policy, which is continually to invade other countries and infringe on rights of sovereignty simply for the cause of democracy?

"So what are you going to do, let the Soviets take over the world, piece by piece?" Parker asks.

I ask the same question, but can only reply that this balance of power play is getting a bit out of hand—particularly when it's so difficult to keep the balance these days. I suppose the idea of laying down our swords first and setting the examples is much too idealistic—but what other alternatives do we have, except for a continuous cold war? While people starve, we build bombs. It just doesn't make any sense.

If we had the guts and didn't care about risking our careers and my marriage and the reputations of our Chinese friends, we would have followed my idea and marched on Saturday at the American embassy to oppose the invasion of Grenada. But we don't have extraterritoriality here (which is actually all for the better), and thus we fall under the Chinese law that says people don't have the right to organize gatherings of the "opposing political policy" nature.

Talked all morning with Larry about it. Christ, we had a chance to fulfill our obligation. But we really couldn't do it. I won't forget this morning and the things we talked about. In the final analysis, Larry is our official leader, and he has the final word. And because I respect him and know that in fact he does have a social conscience and does care about international law and sovereignty, I felt without qualms that his word was final. His wish that the program will not be a political entity is impossible. Perhaps not impossible in the public sphere (and thus no march at the U.S. embassy today), but in private, we are political; everything is. Every human being's mere existence is political. It's true, this invasion makes any of the U.S. criticisms of Afghanistan a joke.

October 31, 1983   *Halloween night. Tomorrow, Hopkins interview.*

Just the beginning. I get glimpses every now and then. We went downstairs to the party, he didn't realize we were going since I hadn't put on a costume. He smiled when he discovered the surprise. And they were all so sweet to him. Each one explaining their costumes, music playing.

"Let's take a picture," someone yelled. Ruo-xin dashed to the side of the room in order to stand out of the way of the picture.

"Ruo-xin, you, too," someone said. I had to drag him over, practically. Dancing, we sat together with the other Chinese and watched. Two of me. One, sitting next to Ruo-xin and sharing in his discovery as he watched with such curiosity. And the other part of me on the floor dancing, moving, enjoying the freedom of celebration. Without him dancing, with him being so new to it all, it just wouldn't have felt right to let go, let it all hang out.

I fear my feelings in anticipation of times like this back home when he's taking years to get accustomed. I fear my resentment and desire for wild parties and dancing to the Go-Gos with Nathan. But all the fear for naught. Because each time I feel so natural, so good sharing the very slow process of acclimation with him. I guess it's because he is such a sweet man-child, because he's my best friend in the world and I respect him so. And he makes me so happy that I want to go along, step by step, with him—no matter what notions I used to have about what I thought my husband would be like.

Pin the spider on the web. It's almost ten o'clock, and we have to leave before the Chinese curfew. As we're walking out, the girl pins the chalk on his jacket (since she's blindfolded). He turns to her and laughs, a huge smile across his face. She laughs. We all smile and cheer. He leans down to give her back the chalk and smile at her blindfolded face. We leave the party and he's still laughing.

"How funny." Ruo-xin said to me. "I wasn't sure what it was. They really know how to party."

He went and got me some hot water from the water house and then said goodbye. A glow on his face, twinkle in his eyes from what he had seen.

Ah, the times in good old Room 200. He said when he came in after studying tonight that perhaps his biorhythms were at the low point today. "Just frustrated." But you sure couldn't tell when he left.

Every once in a while he gets a glimpse of his new world. As much as he still doesn't understand it, he can feel it coming and the anticipation feels good. I can see it in his eyes.

November 8, 1983

Last evening's adventure is one to remember. The Mincers came to Beijing and I went to the State Guest House to meet them. Had a wonderful time, talked until eleven o'clock. Uh oh. No taxis that late. No buses. I called Parker. Radio announcement: Yuri Andropov

missed celebrations of the victory of the revolution. Hmmmm...
Parker went and told Ruo-xin, who rode his bicycle all the way out
there. The busboy walked me to the gate where Ruo-xin was waiting.
I hopped on the back of the bicycle and he rode me home. I sang to
him all the way; the road was empty of all people. Open road, misty
fog, and we rode along, happy to share an unexpected extra hour together.

Congress has approved the production of one hundred new B-1
bombers and the deployment of new MX missiles. Is this a step toward looking for peace? Come on. Do they really believe that?

Saw a Russian-made movie about Stalin and the revolution in
1919. Stalin was depicted as an understanding, warm, brave leader.
Wilson was pictured with other imperialist presidents sittiing on the
floor with a huge map in front of them planning to divide up Russia.

The music. Meant to be serious, but it was hysterically funny.
Dramatic piano in the background as Stalin walks through Red
Square.

Princeton interview tomorrow.

November 12, 1983   *Saturday at midnight*

The Cultural Revolution comes back to Ruo-xin in waves. He became silent tonight. I knew he was fighting it—and then he gave in.
We waited together. He sang me a song that he loves.

Forget the past, my love. But always remember the strength of
friendship you have with your brother.

Many say this new movement, the antispiritual pollution movement, is nothing to fear. Simply be careful and all will go well. But I
can feel it. They're all watching so carefully, waiting, wondering.

I came back home tonight and the blossom had fallen off the
plant in my room while I was gone—and it had been just about to
bloom.

November 13, 1983   *Seven hours later*

Morning is a time to be awake.

Every day I wonder where Liu Mei-chun is. I wonder if she and
her husband have stayed in the West. I can't imagine it; with all their
grievances against China, she especially did not feel comfortable
with the darker sides of American culture.

Could it be that they fear the cleaning out of the Party? It's hard to know what they might be criticized for, but she was quite heavily involved in the rioting during the Cultural Revolution. Maybe they're afraid to come back. I find it hard to believe. More than likely they're with their son in Canton.

This country is crazy. It's so hard to be here sometimes.

It's all alien to me. What pushes me like this out into the world? Why have I put myself into this situation? Didn't I want to explore? Don't I still want to? Yes, but did I know about this. What's happening now? No, I guess not. This is a fear like one I've never known. One that can't be shared with my family back home. They would be struck too deep. And none of these things can go through the mail. Even with Ruo-xin here, I feel alone.

"How do I find the strength to live with it?" I ask myself. And even as I ask, for some reason the strength and courage are there, and each day comes and goes. Something has been growing, learning, constructing inside of me ever since I came here fifteen months ago.

Too vague to pinpoint it today. But the feeling is there—and it is what makes me strong.

I dreamt about the MX missle last night. Stupid world.

November 18, 1983

Five minutes to eight o'clock on Friday. Class begins soon. It's a pleasure to watch them greet one another in the morning. I don't know why they are this way. Grabbing each other around the neck, breaking into big, bright, natural smiles. Unbounded, they express themselves openly with one another (only within the boundary of their own sex, mind you).

I'm enjoying reading *Laughing Boy*. I've never read about the lives of the Navajos before. Makes me think of Peter Drew when he and his family lived with Navajos and helped them work on a typewriter.

Class is starting.

Later that evening: Excellent lecture. Talked about the importance of the human factor in management and economic planning. Perfect timing, just coinciding with my essays.

I went to see Jin Hui tonight. It's been over a year since I saw him last. Time has gone by. I figured it was a good time to see him again; I've been dying to know how his life has been. At first they told me he had been transferred somewhere else. Then I went to another desk to ask, and they told me where to reach him.

At first he didn't recognize my voice over the phone. Then he said, "Basha! It's been a long time since I've seen you. You're still here."

We met for fifteen minutes. His very first words were "It's dangerous for us to meet here." I knew he'd say that. He always was paranoid.

Same sweet smile. Still writing poetry and practicing his calligraphy.

"Let's go to the park on Sunday."

"Jin Hui, I don't think it's a good time."

"I'll give you my address."

"Good, you can send me your poetry. I'll translate it and take it back to America. . . . Jin Hui, I'm engaged."

"Engaged?" His eyes filled with tears. "Congratulations."

"He's Chinese."

"Chinese?! I knew you'd marry a Chinese. I'm glad to see you happy."

We chatted for a while and then said goodbye. He knows, without my saying so, that we shouldn't see each other again. Anyone but him. It just isn't in keeping with custom here. I belong to someone else. Jin Hui wanted to build something more than just the friendship that I was enjoying so much. And finally, politics. All these reasons added up to the sadness of having to say a final goodbye. Still, I was so glad to see him once more. To know he was still spirited and happy and feeling, not hardened by the time past.

When I came to China I had to speak English with Jin Hui because my Chinese was just out of it. But tonight we spoke Chinese—with ease. I fulfilled another goal. It feels good. This showed the contrast too clearly, between then and now, in terms of my Chinese.

"It's too sudden. You can't have learned to speak so well in just a year," he had said.

It is possible. And I did it.

I left the party by half past seven and came home. Wrote Mom and Dad a letter and then went to find Ruo-xin. He was really moved when I told him the story. As a matter of fact, I was surprised at how much he empathized with the whole thing, squeezing my hands tightly and squealing and smiling as I related the conversation to him.

"Of course I'm not angry," he answered when I asked him. "This is the way things are. It's very moving. People are this way. There's nothing to be angry about. I'm just happy that you're happy."

Such a sweet man-child.

I can't believe how much time has passed.

November 20, 1983

I love the morning. It's still my favorite time of day. I like going to bed early enough, ten-thirty or so, so that I can wake up at six-thirty feeling rested and watch the sun rise over Beijing.

Yesterday afternoon Ruo-xin came over at three o'clock. I was still taking my nap (a lazy Saturday afternoon). He slipped into bed with me and then his warm body sliped into mine. Two young bodies eager to touch, to climax together. Mmmm, so good. Finally, we got to work addressing my graduate school stuff. There we sat at the desk by the window. Ruo-xin put on a few of the return addresses and "air mail" in Chinese characters. I knew they'd stamp it just the same at the post office, but I wanted him to feel involved in the process more than just through emotional support. A French novel I had never heard of by Victor Hugo was being performed over the radio in Chinese. Ruo-xin chattered away about the history of the characters, who was "good" and who was "bad" and so on. He was pretty moved by the whole thing.

When everything was all addressed, we put the stuff in the pink flowered shopping bag. No words were spoken. I felt anxious. We know how important these applications are. If I don't get into graduate school, we'll have quite a road to hoe. Basically because I'm not trained to do anything except think and everything Ruo-xin is trained for is still in Chinese. If I get into graduate school we'll really have a chance to shoot for the top; I'll get training and finally a salary that can put Ruo-xin through school in the U.S., once he's ready. If I don't get in, I don't even know where we'll live. China or the U.S. I could do a lot here even without a graduate education, so can Ruo-xin. But I'll always be a foreigner here. Always. Always.

My dream last night was very telling. I dreamt I was on a small ship tossing on a river. Suddenly I was safe on land with Ruo-xin. But before a minute had passed, a policeman came up and questioned us. He took Ruo-xin's wallet as if he were looking for a reason to nail us. In the wallet he found a picture of me superimposed on a picture of mountains and a sunset. My eyes were closed in the picture, head thrown back, hair loose and tumbling down by back.

"This is pornography!" he told us. "You've broken the law. This is spiritual pollution."

He made a phone call. When he had hung up he said, "It wouldn't have been too bad if you hadn't been wearing blue jeans [a sign of evil foreign influence]. But since you're wearing blue jeans and have a pornographic picture, you have to pay a fine of 11,000 RMB." That's $3,500 in the U.S.!

I started yelling at him. "This is a free country! I can wear my jeans if I want without getting fined!"

A free country.

"It's a question of whether we want to live in a free country or in a country without freedom," I told Ruo-xin on the bus yesterday as we were on our way home.

"I know," he said.

"If we have grey spirits and lose our optimism, then we'll never get anywhere," he said later on. It's true.

One evening last April we sat on a bench in the courtyard and decided to change our lives. Just in the space of a minute we opened up a whole new world. It's a world of love, support, and a rare friendship. But it's also a world of uncertainty, fear, and decisions. A world where some would say the odds are against us. I can't completely agree with that, but at the same time the uncertainty of what our future will be, particularly materially, is a big bad question mark.

That's hard to face. But we've faced it. The possibility of not getting into grad school has forced us to confront it.

And what did we come up with? Scared eyes and optimistic words. Afraid but knowing that with each other and positive attitudes, we'll make our way.

It's scary sometimes. But just in time he grabs my hand and gives me his smile. Devoted to each other, we'll be able to make our own happiness.

Remember our motto! We never give up!

Ugh.

November 21, 1983

And there I was, complaining about a stupid yeast infection.

We were watching TV last night when someone in the movie mentioned about how wrong it was to leave one's mother country behind or something to that effect.

I've felt a lot of feelings about this topic ever since Ruo-xin and I decided to get married. Mostly I've felt a lot of self-inflicted guilt. But as Ruo-xin explained to me last night, he resolved it in his heart a long time ago. To live in the States or in China, anywhere, as long as you are building your own life with the one you love.

"We have to start on our own road," he said. "I can't live forever in my parents' house. I have to go out and make my own way."

"But I don't want you to be sad," I said to him.

His reply was that he feels, since he remained positive through the hardest of times, the Cultural Revolution, that he can be positive and strong through anything.

I guess it triggered something inside of him. We got off the bus and walked into the school grounds. As we were going past the main door of the foreign students' dormitory, he began his story.

"When I was seven, during the Cultural Revolution, there was only my mother and myself at home. I remember at one point we had no money left and no food to eat. We were so hungry and wanted some meat. There was a strong wind from Siberia that night. Mama went to the neighbors and begged 2 mao [5 cents U.S.] to buy some meat. Then she gave me the money and told me to go out and buy our dinner. But I . . ."

Suddenly he began to shake. Overcome with grief, he burst into tears. "I lost the money in the wind and returned home with nothing for Mama to eat." He cried for just a moment and then pulled it all back inside.

"Don't worry. It's nothing. I'm OK."

I guess there's nothing else to write after that.

"Things are so much better now for my family. We are much happier. And then I found you. I never gave up hope. I knew life would be better again. And now it is," he whispered to me smiling. "You're so beautiful."

November 22, 1983

I must be the luckiest woman in the world. I woke up this morning at quarter after six before the sun rose and the full moon was right outside my window. Reminds me of the summer I spent in Kampsville, Illinois, when I woke up every morning and the moon was always shining in through my window. It's such a special feeling.

November 23, 1983

I can't believe it. The sweet Japanese girl from Okinawa who I thought was nineteen years old turns out to be twenty-eight. I know she seemed a little more independent than the rest of the Japanese girls, but I never imagined she was twenty-eight. She went to Tokyo University—very impressive; it's the Harvard of Japan. Majored in eighteenth-century literature.

My lungs are unhappy once more. I don't know what triggered it. Maybe the cold air. Who knows? But if drinking lots of this boiled pears concoction worked before, it'll work again. My lungs, my bladder, I'm losing my hair, I mean come on!

Finished my essay for Johns Hopkins tonight after Wu Xiao Ping and I got back from the park. We spent a wonderful windy afternoon wandering around by North Lake park. Wu Xiao Ping, one of many friends who so badly wants to work for the modernization of her country but doesn't believe in communism.

I found Ruo-xin in the classroom after dinner. The room was empty except for him. He stood facing the blackboard, reading his English out loud. Sweet man. If only I had worked as hard in college as you do, I'd get into any grad school I chose.

I hate to be drinking this pear stuff when he comes by to say good night tonight. It seems like I'm always getting sick these past three months. It makes me feel—I don't know—not strong, I guess. I feel strong emotionally, but things keep going wrong in this old body.

They left for Xian today. Sarah, Parker, and Leighton sat in my room for an hour after lunch and we chatted. I haven't enjoyed peers as much as I've enjoyed this bunch here in Beijing this year. They're just bright, straightforward, motivated people and I really love being with them. They enjoy being with me, too; I guess that's part of it.

Sarah is special. Really has her two feet on the ground, even after all she's been through. She enjoys me for who I am, and it's mutual. Now that's a pleasure.

November 24, 1983   *Thanksgiving Day*

The Voice of America brought the news today. Twenty-four

hours ago, the Soviet Union broke off the Geneva arms talks. When will we ever work this out?

I listened to a young man who is a senior at the U.S. Naval Academy in Maryland. Twelve years to the day of his father's death in Vietnam he received his appointment to the academy. He said he feels highly motivated and excited about being at the forefront of the U.S. defense sometime in the future. His father was killed in Vietnam; no doubt he's highly motivated to go out and fight the Soviet fighters and avenge his father's death. This boy is one of thousands of sons or brothers of my generation whose fathers or older brothers were killed in the Vietnam War. They think they're working for peace, but their thoughts will only breed more war. Sometimes I think there's no hope.

If President Reagan chokes on his pumpkin pie tonight, he deserves it.

8:30 pm, Thanksgiving night

Our first Thanksgiving together. He finished in the lab at five and came over. I had just gotten back from the Beijing Hotel, having mailed out my Johns Hopkins application.

We had bean sprouts done in the wok and noodles. Ruo-xin brought salted peanuts and Chinese sausage and chocolate, which he put down in the center of the table that we had made from two footstools.

I actually did pretty well cooking the bean sprouts, beginner's luck. I made too many noodles and by confession discovered that Ruo-xin has the same problem of making too much food. We took pictures to let Mom and Dad see what our Thanksgiving looked like, then we sat down to feast! Feast? Well, we *felt* like it was a feast, anyway. For a couple of poor students, we felt rich—rich in spirit and love.

A day to give thanks. Thinking of the U.S., we can be thankful for our freedom. We can't be thankful for peace because there is none today. And here is China. It's all too obvious that I can't give thanks for freedom here.

But we gave thanks for our families, and gave thanks that we have each other. Sweet loving man.

We talked about the American Indians—the native Americans—
and how they helped the first settlers back in the 1620's. And then
how two hundred years later the white people forgot how the Indians
had helped them and turned on their friends.

Next year, we'll be apart on Thanksgiving. But I'll be with Mom
and Dad. In 1985? I hope he'll have his visa by then, but who knows.
I'm looking forward to giving him a real American Thanksgiving.

December 3, 1983

We're into the final month of the year. I wonder what China will
be like when we come back twenty years from now.

Will they still have horses and donkeys pulling carts through the
streets?

Will there still be bicycles?

Will there still be piles of cabbage lining the streets every fall?

Who will be the new leaders?

Will the responsibility system still exist?

Will the music still be Mickey Mouse, "Red River Valley," the
Carpenters?

What about the bathrooms? Will they still be holes in the ground,
dirty and stinking?

Will English still be mandatory in the schools?

What will the number of students attending the university be?
Higher than the present 10 percent of those graduating from middle
school, of course.

What will happen to the job allocation system?

Will they still be burning coal?

How many law schools will be set up by then?

Will they still have ration tickets for cotton, edible oils, rice, flour,
and sugar?

What will the divorce rate be? Probably won't see any old women
with bound feet walking around the streets.

Will families still be putting such an emphasis on having sons?

What new Western plays will have been staged since the 1983
production of *Death of a Salesman*?

What will the clothing be like? Will it still be the basic drab colors with the bright colors only for the children?

Will the custom still be to have just one boyfriend or girlfriend at a time, and in one's life?

What about respect for elders?

How about the foreigners' hotels? Will Chinese still not be able to enter on their own? Will foreigners still not be allowed to stay in "locals only" hotels?

I know that as the technology level increases in the next twenty years, energy problems, population control, and leadership succession will change China. But what will the change be? What will she be like twenty years from now when we bring our nine-year-old child over to China to live for a few years? I can't wait to see.

Let's see. I saw *Death of a Salesman* last night. That play gets me every time. We all can empathize in some way with what Willy Loman goes through.

I've noticed a big change since I became engaged to Ruo-xin. Watching death scenes, where wife loses husband or vice versa, really affects me. Hurts. I think of a time when he'll be too old to go on and he passes away and I get the strangest feeling inside, as if I won't want to live a day past the day he dies. I guess it's the children that keep you going.

I think of Mom and Dad. Ugh, what a lousy feeling. How many years really do they have left together.

Twenty-five years at most. Maybe thirty. I guess that's a long time, but it goes so fast. How will one exist without the other?

I remember the day I yelled at Daddy for not believing in life after a loved one died. He should be able to be independent. But now I realize, it's not a matter of independence at all. It's a matter of deep, deep love and friendship—of that other person becoming an intricate part of your soul. How can one go on without him or her? Now I understand. It's a sad feeling, even in the midst of the amazing sensation of having found such a love.

I guess it's the children that keep you going after your loved one dies. This is a whole new set of feelings for me.

I went to the Free Market yesterday and bought vegetables for dinner. I felt so good about how my paper was coming together and so high from talking to Mom and Dad on the phone. They sounded so wonderful and responded so positively to all the stuff that I wrote for grad school. Who wouldn't feel great after that? So I decided it was time to celebrate.

Ruo-xin bought rice from the cafeteria and I prepared dinner.

Rice	.15 (U.S. cents)
Vegetables	.35
Oil—negligible	
	.50

Fifty cents for dinner. Not bad. And we thought it was a feast. I did the vegetables myself and Ruo-xin was amazed that I could do it so well without him teaching me. Except I discovered that I had used too much oil when I found oil at the bottom of all the bowls.

He came over after working in the lab and Sarah was sitting in my room telling me about her visit with Christopher Wren and his family. We all chatted for a while and then she went to dinner. In her wonderful affectionate way, which she knows I appreciate, she kissed me goodbye. I saw Ruo-xin grin out of the corner of my eye. He's still trying to figure out American female relationships. But then again, so am I.

After we finished eating, we had some hot water. I poured the water from the thermos into the mug with the unicorn painted on it and gave it to him. He got up, found the plain glass, and poured the water from the mug into the glass.

I laughed.

He laughed.

"Don't laugh," he said, smiling. "I just like the plain glass better, that's all."

We washed the dishes and then at twenty past six I, as a true faithful member of the bourgeoisie, went to the play and he went off to class.

December 14, 1983

It's that time of year again. The Americans are beginning to sing Christmas carols and are hanging Christmas signs and decorations.

After Ruo-xin left tonight, I stood outside the door of my room and looked down the hall to the hanging bells and "Merry Christmas" sign. Someone was playing a record of Christmas carols. "Oh come let us adore him, Christ the lord. . ." It suddenly struck me how Western it is, this holiday. How far it is from the world and culture he knows.

He's so flexible, so open-minded, and naturally willing to bend and explore. But the Western world is so different from China. I'll admit it. Sometimes I'm afraid. I'm afraid to toss him out into the outside world. I've had twenty-two years to learn how to deal with its pressures and I'm still trying to figure out how to cope with it. He's going to have to start the process at age twenty-three. And I know he's going to get hurt along the way. He's so strong—and yet, even the strongest feel the strain when dealing with a new culture, a new world.

All I can do is be supportive with my love. I know how important that is to him. But I'm afraid it won't be enough.

Al's stupid comments in front of other Chinese tonight. Stupid.

"When you get to America . . ." on and on. Making Ruo-xin look like a traitor in the eyes of his fellow countrymen, when in reality he loves China with all his heart and soul. And yet he's leaving. So we can be together. I hope he won't regret it.

December 15, 1983   *4:30 in the afternoon*

The sun is going down and rush hour is happening outside my window.

The rumor found its source in a left-wing magazine called *Zheng Ming*. A young Hong Kong Chinese brought the news and the magazine onto the Mainland (where *Zheng Ming* is outlawed), which is where she told a Japanese student here at Beijing Normal University. Not knowing what to do with the news, the Japanese woman came to my room and after an eon of beating around the bush, whispered the words "Hua Guo Feng tried to commit suicide last week. He didn't succeed. They think it happened after he had a quarrel with Deng Xiao Ping."

Sarah and I called up Christopher Wren and told him what we'd heard. He'd heard it too, but said he couldn't confirm whether or not it was true. A former premier of China tries to commit suicide. Quite a story.

At quarter till one I got on my bicycle and rode over to Ruo-xin's dorm. He was sleeping, as were all his other roommates.

"Ruo-xin, wake up! Wake up! Guess what I heard?!"

"What? Wait, let's go outside."

"They're saying Hua Guo Feng tried to commit suicide."

His eyes opened wide.

"It might be true—and it might not. Don't tell anyone."

December 16, 1983   *Friday, 9:30 am*

I can't believe how rational I'm being. It all started about three weeks ago. The management class had a guest lecturer. Great! The lecture began. We were all pretty up for it. What was the first sentence that came out of his mouth?

"Please, comrades, I request that you not reveal the contents of this lecture to those outside of class. We are still researching the problems I am about to discuss with you. In addition, many of the figures have not been published as of yet."

At which point the professor got up, went over to the podium, and whispered something to the lecturer with an embarrassed smile. Then the lecturer looked out into the crowd, stopped when he found me, and stared for a split second. The whole class turned to look at me. No one said a word.

Then quite nervously the speaker continued with his lecture.

"What should I do?" I asked a Chinese classmate who was sitting behind me.

"I don't know," he said with the same embarrassed smile that the professor had had a moment ago.

I left forty minutes later during break time. Basically, I just didn't want to overstep my bounds. If I become too obvious or cause any discomfort for the professors, they won't let me take any economics classes. This is obviously a situation where they'd rather I wasn't there—even though it's clear that I'm already pretty well aware of some of the serious problems he was prepared to talk about.

I reasoned that for the sake of being able to continue to listen in on economics classes, I would forego this and the following two lectures. (Now I discover that they will continue until the end of this month.)

Ugh! Frustration. But I knew I was stepping into a touchy situation when I started attending these classes. Something like this was bound to happen, and I think I handled it properly.

December 18, 1983   *Sunday morning*

Cathy's off to India! God, how exciting.

"I take comfort in the fact that one day the lives will blend somewhat," I responded to Sarah's question at the party last night around half past eleven.

Her question was, "So tell us, Bess. How do you manage to deal with spending the evening at the Lis' house in a completely Chinese world and then coming home here [Ruo-xin can't come in because it's after ten o'clock] and dancing and drinking with your Western friends?"

I must admit, even before I met Ruo-xin, I've felt the—shall we say "shock"—of being in one world outside the dorm and then an entirely diferent one inside the dorm. In my first five months or so here, it wasn't easy to adjust. It totally flipped me out at times. For the most part, strangely enough, I've enjoyed being able to come back to the safety and familiarity of the sights, sounds, and smells of the dorm: a microcosm of the West plunked down in the middle of a Chinese university.

December 24, 1983

We performed our Christmas play last night. They ate it up again, just like they did last year. Amy turned up at the last minute to come see it. That was a blast from the past. Scrooge was even better this year than last year. And when the little British kids sang the Chinese song at the end, the audience just went crazy. That was fun.

Xiao Ming and Yin Zi came unexpectedly. They were just glowing. They gave me their New Years cards. Xiao Ming really wrote a beautiful one. I've made some good friends here.

Then I hopped on my bicycle and rode back to the dorm to wait for Ruo-xin. He was supposed to come at nine-fifteen and then we'd go off to the party together. Nine-thirty-five and he still hadn't come. Then I heard his footsteps on the stairs.

"Sorry I'm late!"

He had been in the lab and lost track of the time. This has happened a number of times in the past few weeks; I love to see it. When I see him involved, caught up—interested in his work—I get such a good feeling inside. Nothing can replace that.

The night was clear and cold. He drove and I hopped on the back of the bicycle, Chinese-style. We took the back paths over to Gong Number 20 building where the party was. It's a test every time, these parties. It's something totally new for him, and with him there, it's new for me, too. He amazes me every time. As uncomfortable as I know he feels inside in the first few moments, with the help of some friendly people he finds himself relaxed and enjoying.

Steve shooed me away so that I wouldn't translate and he and Ruo-xin talked for forty-five minutes in English. Everyone who meets him and gets a chance to chat with him is captured by his warmth and easy-going manner. Gee—not me!! I never noticed those qualities before! I love to watch him making his way in the crowd.

Then we danced for a while. Dancing isn't easy for the Chinese—Western dancing, that is. But each time he gets a little more relaxed. I can't wait to see him out on the dance floor of a night club in Chicago dancing with Sal. Ugh! Will those times ever come?! It seems like an eon away.

But one day, a year and a half to be exact, the time will have come and gone and the years will be ours to share for as long as life will allow.

December 25, 1983

Another Christmas without snow. I can picture so vividly looking outside my window at home onto a snow-carpeted front lawn. At Christmas Mom and I would listen to Dylan Thomas' "A Child's Christmas in Wales." I wonder if Mrs. Patterson is still playing that film for her students every year at the high school? It's such a gorgeous production.

Wintertime meant early morning breakfasts out in the backyard by the fence. (Was there a fence then?) Daddy made a fire in the snow and we all sat around it and had breakfast and pretended we were camping out. I remember I used to bring my doll to those breakfasts. I wonder what ever happened to her?

Of course I remember all the presents at Christmas. I wonder now why we always had presents at Christmas? Doesn't really make sense for a Jewish family. I guess because that's a parent's real pleasure, to give to their kids and see them happy.

That time passed so quickly.

Wintertime walks in the woods and then coming home to a fire in the fireplace and hot chocolate.

I remember once in high school, coming back from a play practice of *The Prime of Miss Jean Brodie* and falling asleep by the fire, wrapped up in Mom's grey coat—the "blankey".

I think I'm going to have lots of kids. Better be rich then, kiddo, to send them all to college and keep them clothed and fed! Oh, well.

Anyway, Christmas Eve. We (Ruo-xin, myself, Parker, Sarah, Leighton, and Laura) went to a Pakistani restaurant before Leighton left for the train. He really is a wonderful guy. Truly an American, but with a sweetness that the Chinese have. He's so good to people.

Xiao Ming and Yin Zi were talking about that yesterday afternoon. That's Ruo-xin's really strongest characteristic, the one that strikes you first. That he is able to communicate with and be comfortable (likewise, they are comfortable with him) people of all types: rich; poor; high-ranking Party members; construction workers; the good, proper students; and the lazy, relaxed, not-so-bright students. A quality that the late Premier Zhou En Lai had, the reason why his people loved him so and grieved so at his death. It's a rare quality— and one that my family has; thus, it is natural that Ruo-xin should join us.

Anyway, dinner was no great shakes. Too expensive and there was a lot of tension between Sarah and Laura, and Parker and Laura and Sarah and Leighton and Laura, so there wasn't too much conversation. Interestingly enough and much to my surprise, Ruo-xin was the most diligent at trying to keep the conversation going. He told two jokes that cracked me up, but lost something in the translation (as I had to translate it for them). Ruo-xin and I laughed and then felt very uncomfortable to see a table of blank faces who had been unable to understand the joke. If you don't understand this place and the attitudes about the cult of Mao, then the joke doesn't work. The next joke had a bit of a more universal basis and so went over a bit better.

Two years ago I wouldn't have blinked an eye to spend 10 Yuan (about 3 U.S. dollars) on a meal, But I guess there's where I've undergone a real change. It's a supreme waste of money to spend all that just on food. That's one seventh of the average city worker's monthly salary. It really turned my stomach after a while.

Anyway, I was glad to leave and head over to Ruo-xin's parents' house. We found them sitting on the bed, watching TV. The program was typical. Different singers sang songs that originated from various parts of China. While they sang, their heads were put up against pictures of clouds, mountains, etc. Really tacky. But the songs were upbeat and the Lis were enjoying it.

Ruo-xin's father was away in the countryside from the time Ruo-xin was five years old until he was seventeen. His father was allowed to come home once a year. So he was raised by his mother when he was young, and then in his teen years by my favorite—Ruo-ji. Sadly, Mrs. Li harbors a deep resentment for her husband for not being in Beijing from 1966 to '79. As her mind slowly goes, she has forgotten that he was sent to Shan Xi for hard labor and did not go by choice.

Just last night, she exploded into a rage. She cursed him for leaving her alone to raise the children and screamed until Ruo-xin and Ruo-ji succeeded in calming her down. Mr. Li just sat in the chair and said nothing.

Ruo-xin drew some pictures later that evening that I put up on the wall here in my room.

January 2, 1984

What a wonderful New Year. Particularly New Year's Day. New Year's Eve was—well, let's see. It all started off when I asked Ruo-xin on the bus if he would help me get some economics books that weren't normally available to foreigners. "No problem," he said and then we changed the subject. But I felt the vibes after that. He was uncomfortable, worried, troubled.

"You have to be careful," he explained later on that night. "It's easy to get in trouble here. Don't talk too much about your opinions or what material you're looking for with other people. One of my classmates even warned me to tell you not to talk so much."

"You could walk into a situation unknowingly and when the time came for approval of our marriage we wouldn't have a chance. I couldn't bear it if that happened, if I'd have to spend my life without you."

Obviously, I'd already thought about all this over a year ago—and ever since then. I realize what's going on and how to be careful.

But his emotions were stirred and he wanted to stress the importance of this issue.

"Ruo-xin, the deeper I get into this field, the riskier my research will become. If you're afraid, you'd better think twice about our marriage. I won't marry a man who wants to hold back my work—"

At which he broke in, "You know that's not what I want to do. I'm not afraid and what's more I support you in your work. You are a rare person and can do a lot of good for the world. I support you in that effort. Your field is fascinating too me, too! But I only want to be careful. The Communist Party is paranoid and unpredictable. I don't want to lose you."

I explained to him that in the present and near future, none of my research will be of the crucial kind. I haven't even defined my master's thesis yet, though I have a good idea of what it will cover. There's nothing to worry about right now.

"Our relationship is based upon mutual understanding—which is why we have conversations like this. It is also based on mutual support and mutual respect. These are crucial, as they have been in the past and will be even more so in the future. I promise to be careful. I would do nothing that would endanger the chances of us being able to spend our lives together. I only hope that you yourself are truly convinced of your words when you say you support my plans as I support yours. . . . I am nothing without you, now that my life, my heart have become so much a part of yours. But I am also worthless without work that I believe in."

"I know. I respect you for that. That is what is so special about you and that is what I have learned from you. Bai Yu-sha, I can't help but support you in your goals, because your goals are my goals and vice versa. As we have expressed, there is a lack of understanding in the world that we can help to remedy. If we can do our part for bringing together the people of East and West, China and America, we'll be doing what we have always hoped for. And by working for this friendship and exchange between the two countries, we are truly working for their welfare and world peace. You know that these, too, are my goals. Our hopes will be expressed through research, education, work from eight to five o'clock, in our relationship, and in our children. They are the ultimate in unity between our two nations."

We walked for a long time, overcome by the emotions of the evening. Soon it would be 1984, not an easy year for the two of us—but an exciting one.

We never speak of communism as a solution to the world's problems. We know that answers cannot be so black and white. But we do talk about the idea of communism and how wonderful it would be if it could really happen. The problem lies in the method. I don't like the methods that are being used. Ruo-xin has his qualms about it, too. And so we stand in a seemingly unsolvable position. We have asked ourselves, too, "Can people's nature be changed such that their thoughts are truly fitting for the workings of communism?" And if it were possible, how else could the dictatorship (the leading revolutionary party) change the way people think but by control, and thus chipping away at their freedoms until we have nothing but George Orwell's *1984*.

There's another way to look at Orwell's *1984*, as I explained to a literature professor here. He answered that the problem is that the Chinese Communist Party doesn't understand the alternative interpretation, and thus the book is censored here in China. The novel, *1984*, can be seen as a book that doesn't attack communism but actually hopes for it. The writer uses his pen to speak out against totalitarianism. Against the power of government over innocent citizens. Whereas if there existed true communism, there wouldn't even be a state. There wouldn't be need for any government at all.

But my fears are, and they have been confirmed here in China, that the way to try to reach the ideal (the only method we can visualize, the ultimate ideal which incidently because of its nature and because of some man's desire to dominate others and hold power, will never happen) is through a dictatorship, a Big Brother–type society, a lack of freedom and thought control. I hope China can find another way. I think it's a futile hope.

Anyway, where was I?

After a nice long walk, we came back to the house and saw the new year arrive.

But earlier in the evening, we got Mama and Ba Ba going on about the family's prerevolution history. It turns out that the family held offices in the Qing Dynasty government. And there must have been some Manchus in the clan. Ugh. Another scar on the family record.

His mother described how they all lived together—a huge extended family on a big plot of land. Forty families. She described going to the Buddhist temple ceremonies, "laying incense and bowing down to the Gods." She giggled. "There was always a lot to eat and we grew all kinds of vegetables." They were landlords.

Then the Communists came and everyone was scattered. The Japanese invaded the North where they were living, and life became hard. I'm not sure if it happened right when the Communists came in the thirties, or postrevolution, but the land was divided up. Those of the family that survived scattered around the country from North to South. Many went to work on the railroads.

When I come back in August 1985, Mrs. Li and the others want to take a trip up North to her original home. That would be an exciting trip.

After a huge dinner, Ruo-ji, Ruo-xin, and I went for a long walk down Wang Fu Jing Street. Sweet Ruo-ji, he will be a fine husband for someone one day. If he ever can find a woman who is as wonderful as he.

After midnight came and went, we all got ready for bed. Mrs. Li and I in one room, the three boys in the other room. Thick blankets and foot warmer bottles filled with boiling water kept us warm. Soon the lights went out and I looked around me.

Amazing. Lying here in a Chinese home. I guess I found my way to penetrate what many foreigners have called an "impenetrable society." And soon they will be my relatives.

Mrs. Li talked in her sleep, called out "Ruo-xin!" It's hard to believe she has lived through the Japanese invasion, the fall of the Qing government, the Communist take over, the famine from 1961 to '63, and the Cultural Revolution—and bore six kids, two of whom died. What a history.

"Are you warm enough, Bai Yu-sha?" she asked me.

"I'm as warm as could be, Mama. Sleep well."

"Sleep well."

The house (two rooms) was crowded for sleeping so many people. But it was cozy. "Everyone together" kind of feeling.

We got up the next morning and made the beds. Washed our faces one at a time in the basin set down in the bedroom.

Breakfast, which Ruo-xin didn't eat—he's not a breakfast eater—was good.

Then off to the Beijing Hotel at nine-thirty to call the family for their New Year's Eve. That was exciting. Everyone was there. Daddy commented how much China is changing—as he can see from the articles I send home. It's true. Pretty nifty to be here right now. But what will the change lead to? Mom said time will pass more quickly than ever.

Linda left early to go back to New York; Joey sounded more angry than sad. That's good. Sal and Pete. I felt like they were standing right next to me. Peter asked to talk to Ruo-xin. What a riot!

"Hello?" Ruo-xin said in a soft, nervous voice. "I am Ruo-xin. You are Peter? Happy New Year."

What a scream!!

And he talked to Mom, too.

"Hello, Ruth. I am glad to hear [your] voice."

Then he couldn't understand what she was saying so he gave the phone to me.

"Take good care of Bessie," she was saying.

He does. He certainly does.

Back home for a big lunch. Lamb. Mongolian-style. And wine. And then a nap.

When Ruo-xin and I woke up, the Li family was in the next room watching TV.

We got ourselves together and went back to school around half past two. What a wonderful new year.

January 5, 1984

The more I read about communism, the less I believe in it. "When the higher phase of communism is attained, all minds in everyday life will be supplied by the collective means of society. Children will be raised and educated by society, and the family will be relieved of these economic functions. Only then will there be no more contradiction between social collective labour and the household work of the individual." (Xue Mu Qiao)

Forget it.

January 6, 1984

I guess I've been lucky that it's been so smooth for so long. But as Ruo-xin said, I was bound to discover what I did yesterday. Unfortunately, it has put a very sour taste in my mouth about China and politics here and people's narrow-mindedness. Political racism.

It's more than likely that the movement going on now (which has been likened to 1965) is the reason for what really is a change in attitude by some of my friends and acquaintances. They're afraid. Christ, I could scream.

This is what happened. Li Hua said to me after lunch yesterday, "Bai Yu-sha, you'd best not talk about political issues with Li Ruo-xin. If he receives your influence and others can tell that he has, or if his comments in conversation reveal that he has, it will be bad."

At first I didn't know how to respond. I was amazed. My influence? I can imagine the government fearing my influence on people, but a classmate? A person on my level, someone just like me, who I thought I was friends with, says my influence is bad?

"Are you trying to tell me what I should and shouldn't talk about with Ruo-xin?"

"Only for now. Once the two of you are out of China, it's fine. But here, with the anti-spiritual pollution movement going on, you should be careful."

"I know we have to be careful. We are careful."

"You should understand what I'm saying to you. You should know already. Don't let them see that he has received your influence and there won't be any problem. So don't talk about politics with him."

"At least, I shouldn't express my point of view?"

"Right."

"I'm tired. I'll see you."

"Bye!"

Bitch. As I said to Ruo-xin later that day, I hope she never gets out of this country. And that's quite a curse.

Ruo-xin and I discussed the issue as we walked out on the athletic field. It was cold and cloudy. Grey. The ground crunched hard and dry beneath our feet. I really just want to leave this place and these people. If they want to have a spiritual pollution clean-up movement, let them have it without me. They say they welcome us here, but they don't welcome us as we are. They fear our thoughts, our opinions, our actions, everything that makes us who we are.

It's really not a new lesson learned. Bring your technology and your capital, but don't bring your politics and ethics. I knew the government felt that way. But I thought the people felt differently. What happened to this huge separation betweeen government and people that all the Chinese talk about?

"Things are different since August, when the anti-spiritual pollution movement started," Ruo-xin tells me.

I know, I'm not blind.

"We can't talk about true feelings or opinions, with our families these days. There's a movement going on and everyone is being careful. They're scared. That's why Li Hua said what she said to you. She wants you to be careful."

"I know. I understand."

Sometimes I hate this place. There absolutely is no freedom of thought. That's not new to me. Only just now I realized that the people are still victims. They say their attitudes toward the government have changed since the Cultural Revolution.

"We obeyed too easily. Now we know. Now we have our own opinions."

But this is the way of life in a socialist country. When a movement comes, opinions go under the carpet and they do exactly as they're told. Just like they said they *wouldn't*. Another cultural revolution is possible. Because it's people like this who have no guts to change their situation, who allow themselves to be oppressed by the supreme oppressors.

International relations with this country is going to take some very skilled people. It requires utmost talent. I hope I can be a part of it.

I don't understand how Ruo-xin survives here. His thinking is so different from most of them. He's going to blossom in the U.S.A. What an amazing mind to think the way he does, amid all this oppression.

This country is a sad story.

So now I close my mouth. Not one opinion will breathe from my lips. I'm no fool. I don't want the government to nail me or my man. But when I leave, you bet I'll tell the world what's going on here.

January 6, 1984 *continued 5:00*
  at Ruo-xin's house

Mama's making clothes on the table. A warm cotton jacket to keep her cozy in these cold rooms.

Today added another to the list. Jake came into the dining hall today at around half past eleven. His face was ashen.

"I saw it. I saw it with my own eyes," he whispered. "I can't believe it. I thought they were going to beat him to a pulp right before my eyes."

And then he told us the story. A man who had apparently stolen two blankets was on the run and the Public Security Bureau caught him on the street (on school grounds). No problem, they caught him. Fine. But after they caught him, they started to beat him. Then they made him put his bicycle on his back ("like a cross," Jake described) and took him down the road, continuing to beat him.

They're really cracking down.

No justice. Just catch the thieves and beat them.

Innocent until proven guilty? Forget it. You're behind bars before you can blink an eye. Sentenced within days, and afterwards executed without a chance for a plea for forgiveness.

That's how the law works here. Terror.

January 8, 1984   *Saturday morning*

Last night Ruo-xin came back to the house all aglow. They had watched an American film in class about the brain. It featured the latest American technology for brain analysis. He couldn't believe how clearly he could see the brain through computers, etc. He described how everyone was oohing and aahing throughout the film. He said he was careful and serious, keeping the excited emotions inside. Li Hua had her head on her desk. Too bad, honey, you'll never use that technology in your entire lifetime. Actually, that's really sad.

Ruo-xin was bursting. He's itching to see it all for real. I wonder if his job will be in the medical field. It's hard to tell. He goes wacky over plants, too. And animals even more. We'll see. As I was before, I continue to enjoy his hope and excitement about his career. With hard work, long years, and patience, I know he will find what he wants.

China has just joined the International Atomic Energy Agency.

Leighton commented to me yesterday that perhaps Li Hua was just looking out for us, and that she made the comment out of caring. Probably. I should be more understanding. Ruo-xin and Larry are wondering if one of their professors didn't ask Ruo-xin to say something to me in order to caution us. Knowing the system here, that could be quite likely.

January 10, 1984   *Tuesday morning*

Well, let's reevaluate just a bit. Going home to the Ruo-xin's house Friday night helped put things in a little better perspective. As oppressed as they are, inside the Chinese are opinions covering all ends of the spectrum. It's still true, I have to be much more careful about what I say now that the movement has heated up, but it doesn't mean all Chinese look at us as a piece of walking spiritual pollution and political peril.

Do you forget how many Chinese inside and outside the school walls are itching for political freedom, to say nothing of literacy and other artistic freedoms?

The Chinese are not all Li Huas. Those that are, well, you've got to learn how to survive them.

January 16, 1984

Christ, I can't believe it's already the sixteenth! My life is going just too fast.

A beautiful letter from Mom and Dad to Ruo-xin arrived today. I'll tell you, with all the craziness going on, there sure are some nifty people around. I used to think they were so cruel for sending me off to be tortured by the kindergarten teacher, Miss Heidi, at Braeside. Little did I know, I had the best parents in the world. And this is the test: when the kid brings home some "unknown" from a developing country and says, "This is the man I've chosen to be my husband." It takes quite a parent to know the secret delicate balance between too much opposition and not any at all.

Anyway, we sat in an empty classroom after he got back from the lab and read the letter. I was surprised and encouraged at how little he needed my help in translation. He absolutely glowed as he read it.

Ugh! How wonderful!

I want to go home!

No, tomorrow starts the most exciting project since you've come to China. The tutoring sessions with Professor Cai begin tomorrow at eight o'clock. I have presented to him a list of some of the more touchy problems of China's economic development. We will cover that list at the tutoring sessions. I'm really itching for that. This is a rare opportunity that came my way simply because I opened my mouth and asked. So I can't escape yet. Another project is yet to be finished.

January 28, 1984

Vacation. Amen.

Still, if Ruo-xin were not here I'd go up a wall. My professor is fabulous in terms of getting me the information I need, but this whole "Guan xi" bit that goes along with it really makes me sick. Ah, well. The fact that he's taking the time to teach me means that I have to take the time to go to the Friendship Store with him, to listen to him brag about all the high-level muckety-mucks he's so close with. Ugh. Make me puke.

In the U.S., it's a different story. Teaching is teaching. Friendship, if it follows naturally, is wonderful—but it's an entirely different matter. The two don't necessarily have to go together as they do here.

At the railroad station yesterday, Sarah's worker-friend got nailed. They were sitting down for a while to chat after Sarah bought her ticket, when a police officer walked up to them and asked what they were doing. Before they knew it, the policeman had taken the worker to a private room for questioning. Sarah had to wait across the street from the station. Forty-five minutes later he emerged. He was interrogated about his relationship with Sarah (they are simply friends, nothing else). Finally, they even called his unit and reported "the incident." What incident? He was sitting on a bench with an American. I've read the law book, there's no rule that says Chinese can't hang out with foreigners.

But that makes no difference. They suspect the Chinese worker will be infected by American ethics and ideals. (What they really fear, deep inside, and what they should fear, is that with an exchange of ideas and lives, their people will become discontent with the kind of Chinese socialist totalitarianism that exists here and will overthrow the government. But that will never happen here. With some semblance of equality and everyone being well-fed, they're not about to revolt.)

The movie the other day left a strong impression on me. In line with what he had been taught by his father—to do what was best for the good of the country—his son felt, as did most youth of that age, that the Communist Party was the only hope of dragging China out from the depths of feudalism, drastic inequalities between the classes, mass starvation, and exploitation. At the time I'm sure I would have felt the same way. The old society was a cruel, black, heartless place. The struggle of the Communist Party and the youth of that time is well-justified, I believe.

But the richness of the culture, the color and custom—it is a sad thing, that all that has been lost. I'm not refuting the amazing improvements this country has made since 1949. But I, along with many old people I know here, miss the richness of the old society.

Freedom? "Didn't they have freedom then?" you ask. "Look at them now! They can't even sit in the train station without a permit, lest they get hooked by the authorities."

Yes. They had a kind of freedom then. Freedom to leave the

country, if one had the money. Freedom to struggle, freedom to prosper, freedom of thought, religion. But with corrupt government and a terribly stratified class system, the freedoms they had were worthless. Freedom and liberty gone bad. Which is what the United States hopes to prevent. That is our struggle, one objective, continuous forever, a process of checks and balances. And along with the bad men, we have people who believe in reform and law that will protect the economic, political, and social freedoms of the people. I'm not saying the system is perfect. Far, far from it. We have a lot to learn from Marx and Engels and Hagel. But our system today beats socialism on every score, except for security. And we are willing to give up a little security for the sake of pursuing freedom and for the sake of being able to protect the freedoms in any way we see fit. The freedom to reform.

This is not to say that the status quo is king. Far from it. I believe in change to fit the changing times and conditions. I do not believe, however, in supporting a status quo that has seeds of *1984* in its soil.

February 3, 1984

He didn't mean it the way I took it. But I can't go and buy expensive vases when he tells me how China has areas where people still don't have enough food to eat. He simply meant it as a comparison, but it makes me feel terribly guilty. And I'm helpless to solve the problem of inequality, at least for today. The only thing I can do is simply not buy and just get on the bus and go home. Which is what we did. He was upset because his words didn't include the meaning that I gave them (which seems to be the basis of all arguments). I was upset because he was stupid enough not to think before he spoke about what those words might mean to someone of middle-class bourgeoisie, who wishes we could find equality without suffering through the revolutionary, totalitarian, dictatorial methods that seem necessary to create a society of people who are truly equal— economically, that is. The goal of equality is impossible, anyway, and thus makes my position even more uncomfortable and the guilt even harder to bear, considering it is eternal.

Economic equality is impossible because human beings are innately selfish. They want no more then the best for themselves and their families. Some might even feel badly that the family down the street has nothing to eat, but very few would be willing to give half their salary every month and lower their own standard of living drastically for the sake of another human being. The only method to implement equality is through intensive education and thought-training under the guidance. And that doesn't work, either.

February 15, 1984

That's hysterical. An ice skater competing at the Winter Olympics made the comment after being overwhelmed by the ovation from the audience, who he said was largely American: "It sounds funny, but I'm proud to be an American."

That epitomizes the American people's feelings about their country.

February 21, 1984

If I remember correctly, this is Leslie Kahn's birthday. She's twenty-three today. I guess she's still in New York City, pursuing the theatre career that I was meant for but was unwilling to pursue. I wonder how she feels today? What are her feelings as she looks back on her college years? Is she rethinking those years now, as I am? What will she do today to celebrate? Does she ever think of me? Does she remember the times we spent together with fondness? I hope so. I do.

What's the difference between communism and anarchy?

February 28, 1984

Last night was another interesting discussion with Pan Hong. He's received a strong influence from the foreign literature he's read. Particularly evident when he discusses his hopes for change and reform. Granted, there has been quite a bit of change compared to pre-Cultural Revolution. People aren't as ignorant or naive. But they still don't have the rights they deserve. Pan Hong has learned to live with it but knows it could be better.

"Change must be faster, bigger," he dreams aloud.

"Too fast won't work, either," I remind him.

"We already have capitalism here; there's hope!" he says laughing. "Sure, communism is a beautiful, idealistic vision. But how to get there? And is it even possible to implement it? Will it ever be possible? We're all wondering that now."

Went out walking with Ruo-xin at ten o'clock. His mind is on the U.S., and on what he'll do there.

March 2, 1984

Woke up on a Saturday morning, turned on the radio, and what was playing? A song from the Shandong Province called "Family Planning is Good"! And after that came on a song called "Pay Attention to New Reforms"! This country is hysterical.

March 5, 1984   *Monday morning*

I was going to sit down last night and record my feelings of respect for the Chinese people and their struggle. Last night my feelings really came to a head. But I got home late and tired, so instead, I went to sleep. And this morning I have something else to write, so last night goes unrecorded. I hope I have a chance to write it out soon.

Voice of America had a special on the "iron curtain" speech that Churchill gave after World War II. As I listened, I sat back and recalled junior year. As hard as it was emotionally, it was a fabulous year academically. I felt the thrill of contrasting schools of thought in the analysis of (1) American foreign policy and (2) Soviet foreign and domestic policy. The two classes were taught by professors who differed significantly in opinion on the U.S.-Soviet relationship and how it had been handled in the past. One, a revisionist. The biggest thrill of that semester was digesting the lectures, readings, and in-class debates on this important subject. The comparing and contrasting of ideas when it really makes a difference is the most exciting thing life has to offer.

Being here in China has made the notion all the more clear in my mind. For two reasons. One is the value I feel so strongly about sharing and comparing ideas with the Chinese. Although this process has been severely curtailed this year, it has by no means dried up entirely, as is exemplified by my discussions with my Chinese friends, Ruoxin and his family, and a few others. And number two, because I realize, by talking to Chinese classmates and by taking history and economics classes at the university, Chinese education is not only dated, but virtually void of the kind of opportunity I had in the States to wander through the avenues of dissension, disagreement, and opposition, which is sadly oppressed in China.

March 7, 1984

Ruo-xin's birthday. He's twenty-two today. (Wouldn't you know, I'd have to catch the flu just in time for his birthday.)

We went to the ruins of Yuan Ming Yuan yesterday afternoon. Gorgeous weather. We rode our bicycles out into the countryside. As we rode along, we felt the feeling that we move time, the thrill that this is actually real. That there is a person who means so much to me, that this precious *ami* is now a part of my life until we die. Riding down the dirt lanes, chickens and cows and children running everywhere, we looked at each other and laughed. It's too good to be true. With all the hard times ahead, it's still too good to be true.

Walking through the ruins a young couple asked us if we would take their camera and take a picture of them. They stood there against the pillar and as the young man proudly put his hand on her shoulder, the young woman blushed. Snap. Sweet picture.

It's interesting to note that as compared to a year ago, young people are making it a habit not to call each other *comrade* (when asking for directions, assistance, etc.), but are frequently calling each other *Shi Fu*—which literally means "Master." I asked Ruo-xin about it as he asked a young man to take a picture of us and said, "Excuse me, Master. . ." He explained that *Shi Fu* has no "political smell" whereas *comrade* definitely carries the scent of politics.

He'll be here in an hour. I can't wait. When he comes, everyone is going to burst in the room with cake and sing "Happy Birthday." I know that will bring a big smile.

Fever 101 degrees Fahrenheit.

Give me a break!!

March 12, 1984

I can't concentrate on a thing today as I sit here and wait for three o'clock to come. Today we have our meeting with the officials of the school to begin the proceedings for our marriage. I can hardly believe it.

We leaned against the tree out behind the dorm this afternoon and reviewed the list of questions we would ask this afternoon. Ruo-xin wrote them out, grasslike characters on the page. Sometimes I stand back in amazement: I am marrying a Chinese. Who would believe that the lifelong friend of her life, who she would eventually call her husband, would be a Chinese? Chinese, Indian, American, the man in the moon. It makes little difference. What matters is that he is Ruo-xin. His spirit and support and love are irreplaceable. His happiness is my happiness and mine is his. That is what matters.

I am the luckiest woman in the world.

9:30 pm

Things went very smoothly, except that Zheng didn't show up on time and I coughed so hard at one point during the meeting that I had to leave the room. But the procedure is fairly clear now and I understand the forms I have to arrange and the letters I need written in the States.

Ruo-xin handled the whole thing so well. Carefully, businesslike, and yet in a very typically Chinese fashion: not too pushy, setting a question aside when Zheng didn't answer it directly, only to come back to the same question later but in a different form. He was smooth and unhurried, with a strategy in mind and yet a beautiful flexibility that we have only the bamboo to thank for. For once I felt giddy and a little unsure of my sentences. I'm glad Ruo-xin was there to steer that trip.

By the time it was over we were all smiles, all three of us. This won't be easy, but with patience we'll live through it and everything will work out.

After the meeting, Ruo-xin and I went out for a walk in the lovely spring afternoon weather. We sat on the stone fence and reviewed the past hour, pleased with the outcome. How can we go back to our rooms and study now? We asked ourselves. It was already four o'clock, anyway, so we decided to go out for dinner to a nice little restaurant at Hou Hai. We went there for our engagement celebration with Dianne and Aaron last year around this time. Not enough chairs, but we took some from the second floor. Chatted about last summer, about the year coming up, and enjoyed ourselves. The food wasn't as good as last year. Rode our bicycles at dusk beside the lake and felt as if the world were ours. And so it is.

I finished *Spring Moon* tonight. That's an amazing novel. It really succeeds in giving the reader the true taste of change from old China to new China and the life of one woman (born in 1870) who saw it happen. Just amazing.

March 14, 1984,   *Wednesday evening*

Went looking for Ruo-xin at the classroom building. He wasn't there, so I went to his dorm.

Only Zhou Biao was there. I arrived at seven o'clock, left at half past nine. Zhou Biao is the eldest of five. His father is a translator—of Russian. Accused of being a rightist in the Cultural Revolution and severely punished. Zhou Biao's mother was ill for many years and they had to borrow a lifetime of funds to pay. His eyes moistened and he bit the sides of his cheeks as he spoke.

What he really wants to do is to go abroad to study biology. I don't think he'll ever get there. But he studies very hard. It's interesting to hear him talk about how he respects the American youth, hard working and independent. I rarely hear that from the Chinese.

The one biology book written in English is nearly impossible to borrow from the library. Note: must remember to send him one when I get back to the States.

"I hear your New York library has thousands of books," he says, eyes wide.

"Yes."

"And here we are publishing this," he says throwing the selected works of Deng Xiao Ping on the floor. "Look at all this good paper. Simply for his prestige. Thousands of copies. And not enough biology books."

It just doesn't make sense.

I must admit, I really have the strength to do just about anything. I have realized this not only through past experiences, but also recently by seeing myself come out from under an ocean of depressed feelings that came about as a result of the social and political changes this year in China.

Something deep inside of me took charge and showed me that even in the hardest and most unfamiliar of circumstances, I can come through feeling positive, hopeful, and productive—tinted with a welcome sense of realism. Pessimism will never be my brother. I hope my children will find that same sense of strength in their lives. With Ruo-xin and myself as parents, the odds are in their favor. Yet I know, we can only help them find that strength indirectly through our love and support. The essence of the ability to combine realism with optimism will have to come from within themselves alone.

March 17, 1984   *Saturday*

I woke up this morning and could barely believe it. It's really true; I was accepted to Princeton's graduate program at the Woodrow

Wilson School of Public and International Affairs. The letter arrived yesterday afternoon. Even as I sit here, I can hardly believe that this chance is really mine.

Ha! All that hard work paid off!! It's quite possible that I'll really go, when it comes down to my final decision, but we'll see. If Johns Hopkins also accepts me, we're going to have quite a decision to make.

However I finally decide, I think the fact that I have reached this level will give my children even greater encouragement and just that much more of a chance to realize *their* dreams as well. I couldn't ask for anything more. My unborn children, you are so lucky. Even with her faults, you have quite a mother—and she's on your side. And even more than that, your daddy is a gem.

I went running across campus to find him after I called Mom and Dad. I saw him walking past the cafeteria in front of the water house.

"Ruo-xin! I got in!"

His face lit up as he snatched the acceptance letter out of my hand and tried to read it.

"Wonderful!" he shouted.

He caught himself, realizing we were in public as he just about grabbed me up into his arms.

"I knew it," he said. "I was sure you'd get in!"

Sweet love. We walked around and Ruo-xin glowed. He knows that this makes a big difference for our future. After he prepares, he'll be able to attend whatever school he wants because as a Princeton graduate, I'll have a decent job when I graduate. And he knows he'll have a truly career-fulfilled wife.

He decided that we had to go out for dinner. And so we did.

In the afternoon, I washed my hair, chatted with a few people and then went to tell Wu Xiao Ping. She was still sleeping, as were the rest of her roommates. "Xiao Ping," I whispered in her ear. "I got into Princeton!"

"All right! You did it!"

She opened up her blanket and I climbed in. We snuggled up warm and giggled and chatted while everyone slept. Finally her roommates woke up and they were all excited.

"Don't forget us!" they cried as I left a little while later.

That's a Chinese thing to say.

I tutored the Japanese businessman at three o'clock and then left with Ruo-xin. We hopped on our bicycles and floated off down the road.

"Here's to you, Babe, and may this opportunity help you realize your goals. I wish you great progress!" Ruo-xin toasted.

We had a tasty dinner of fish, and hot spicy meat and peanuts and pork. We barely drank a bottle of beer but both of us felt dizzy. Riding out in the cool air, we felt too good.

Work hard, my love. "I will, Bess. Slowly but surely we'll work it all out. Luck is on our side, see! Today proves it. Add to this our hard work and determination and our love, Bessie, and we'll be fine."

We walked around for a long time talking. It was a beautiful evening.

You bet! The world is ours!

March 18, 1984

So now I begin to think about what I want to do, what I want to study, and work after graduate school. The last two years I've been running around saying I have no idea what I want to do, no direction (within the realm of one field, international relations). But that's a lie. I know exactly what I'm interested in. My interest in economics and Third World development is simply an outgrowth of my original, true interest: that of U.S. foreign policy and its impact on Third World development. The classes I've done the best in and enjoyed the most, the books I'm most willing to read, the topic I'm most happy to discuss, the thing that concerns me most is this.

March 25, 1984

I can't bear to leave.

March 28, 1984   *Wednesday morning*

A beautiful run. Gorgeous weather.

Sat in the office last night with Ruo-xin and Blinky and chatted. The two years here, the changes that have taken place and the exciting times ahead. I still can't believe I got into Princeton. Yet I wonder where I'll actually choose to go in the final analysis. Anyway, as hard as it is to leave here, there's the chance to do something I've always wanted to do, to pursue, waiting for me back in the States. It's drawing me home. But my heart. My heart will remain here in China with my beautiful man.

Ruo-ji took us out for roast duck at noon yesterday. We three couldn't have been happier sitting there, chatting, feeling so alive and amazed that we'd all found each other and felt so good together. And yet sad because we know the time we'll be able to spend together (all three together) will become less and less as our lives go on. Ruo-xin and I are going to bring him to America one day to visit. After all he's done for us, for Ruo-xin, for the family, he deserves it.

It just goes to show that there are people among us who are truly model comrades who truly can give of themselves for the good of others. The rest of us would do well to take a lesson from people like Ruo-ji.

April 2, 1984

The Chinese countryside is passing before my eyes once again as the train takes me further and further down south. I slept fairly well last night, which is astounding, considering my state of mind and heart. It was a very sad, tearful goodbye. My dearest man, I will think of you everyday. Even as I make my way down to Canton, I have already begun to wait until I can ride the train back up to Beijing. From that time on, my love, I will never leave your side. It's clear that being apart is too painful to go through it more than once.

This is going to be a long year.

Just about two years ago, I was riding this train up to Beijing with no idea of what was waiting for me. I can't believe the time has come and gone. What an amazing experience.

6:00 pm, the same day

I sat in the bottom bunk with a Norwegian girl who's traveling through the Far East (for lack of anything else to do since she can't find work back in Norway). We ate sausage, preserved tofu, and apples.

Meals. A daily thing. Even meals will be different now. Eating with Americans is different from eating with Chinese. That's an understatement. Wu Xiao Ping. Smiling faces and chattering. Bowls of rice and cabbage. Music in the Chinese scale. I will miss those friends. That relaxed feeling.

What will it be like to live back in the West again?

April 3, 1984   *Evening*

And here I am, passing my traditional one night at the Liu Hua Hotel in Canton. It was terribly depressing this afternoon, but I feel in a bit better spirits now, after having a quick dinner with some enthusiastic tourists. Tomorrow the second leg of the journey, Hong Kong.

It's green, warm, and humid down South; a nice change from Beijing's dry, cold weather (though it did rain for an hour just before I left on the night of April first). It's wonderful to be able to sweat as I jump rope as opposed to getting simply a cold nose and frozen fingers.

Sarah gave me Bettleheim's *The Informed Heart* to read on the trip home, but I can't seem to keep my attention focused on it for long periods of time.

Talk about up in the air. Here I am, I have to be apart from Ruo-xin for sixteen months, I have no idea what to focus on in graduate school (or at least which of the two roads to choose, to be more specific), no summer job.

Courage, my girl. Just think of it as another exciting adventure. And it will be. And to finally get back to school where I've been itching to go for so long. Added to that, if I exercise every day, I think I'll stay fairly sane and happy.

April 4, 1984   *6:30 am*

In the humid morning air of Canton, I wait outside the door for the train that crosses the border into the land of the free. The doors haven't opened up yet. I'll just sit here and wait. The taxi driver who brought me here, forever unable to cross, turned his car around and drove away, back toward the center of town.

There's a man doing Tai Ji Quan over by the wall. A familiar site soon to be left behind. A peaceful, serene, slow kind of feeling that rules the lives of the people on this side of the world is easy to see in his movements. Exercises finished, he walks past me toward the gate where he'll work the day shift.

I don't want to go. If only Ruo-xin would appear right now, right here to take me back with him to Beijing. But that's a dream. In 1982 I came in through this gate to the Mainland, and today I'll pass through again.

It's time to go home, Spero.

Epilogue

Bess Spero Li returned to China in August 1985. She and Ruo-xin were married in September and spent the year living with Ruo-xin's parents in their apartment on the east side of Beijing. Ruo-xin received his first taste of the United States when he and Bess moved to the U.S. in July 1986. After Bess received her master's degree from Princeton in 1987, she returned to China and began working as a consultant at the Beijing office of an American investment consulting firm. Ruo-xin remained in the United States where he currently is working on his PhD at Princeton. Bess returned to the United States and Ruo-xin in summer 1988. They are now together living in Princeton, New Jersey.